fresh encounter

Life Way Press®
© 2009 G. Richard Blackaby, Henry T. Blackaby, and Claude V. King
Second printing 2011

ISBN 978-1-4158-6687-0
Item 005189421

Dewey decimal classification: 269
Subject headings: SPIRITUAL LIFE \ EVANGELISTIC WORK \ REVIVALS

To order additional copies of this resource: write to LifeWay Church Resources Customer Service;
One LifeWay Plaza; Nashville, TN 37234-0113; fax (615) 251-5933; phone toll free (800) 458-2772; order online at
www.lifeway.com; e-mail *orderentry@lifeway.com*; or visit the LifeWay Christian Store serving you.

Printed in the United States of America

Leadership and Adult Publishing
LifeWay Church Resources
One LifeWay Plaza
Nashville, TN 37234-0175

Table of Contents

HENRY BLACKABY is founder and president emeritus of Blackaby Ministries International, an organization built to help people experience God. He travels throughout the world to aid churches in reviving their love for God and lead believers to sense God's call upon their lives.

RICHARD BLACKABY is president of Blackaby Ministries International and the oldest son of Henry and Marilynn Blackaby. During his ministry, he has served as a pastor, seminary president and presently travels extensively to lead believers into a deeper relationship with God.

CLAUDE KING is the discipleship specialist at LifeWay Christian Resources.

An Invitation to a Fresh Encounter with God

There is much joy and hope associated with "beginnings." The birth of a new baby, a new romance, a wedding, a new job ... But we don't live in a perfect world and inevitably life unfolds in ways we had not anticipated. Too often the journey that began with such hope and promise can be spoiled by sin. Parents become estranged from their children, couples split up, a family is torn apart by divorce, a job degenerates into drudgery. But there is always the hope of a second chance. Isn't it wonderful when life offers a chance to get it right? When reconciliation occurs? When broken relationships are healed?

Most people who become Christians experience tremendous excitement and joy as they enter into an amazing, loving relationship with Almighty God. In those early weeks of their salvation, new Christians devour God's Word and excitedly learn to pray with God and worship Him. But the world we live in is a broken world. Believers are not exempt from the challenges of the economy, pain of disease, struggles in our relationships, and effects of sin. Some Christians begin to feel as if God is distant from them and wonder where the vibrancy of their faith has gone. They may continue to regularly attend worship, live moral lives, and serve in their churches, but God seems distant. As a result, many churches are filled with professing Christians who are not experiencing the power of God in their lives. Today's world is in a spiritually deplorable condition. The primary reason is not because of the morally deadening influence of the media, corruption in business, or the lack of godly leaders in government but is due to the fact that there are lifeless, powerless churches dotting the landscape which are making little difference for God's kingdom.

Contemporary believers wonder why the mighty movements of God recorded in Scripture and Christian history are noticeably absent today. Today's pastors are burning out at epidemic levels as they experience the demoralizing futility of attempting to lift their church members out of their spiritual lethargy. While some individuals and churches are experiencing a fresh wind of God's Spirit, many others are asking, "Is there a word from the Lord? What does God want us to do?" Throughout history God has always had a response for those who sought Him. "Call to Me and I will answer you and tell you great and wondrous things you do not know" (Jeremiah 33:3).

But across America and around the world, God's people are crying out for a fresh encounter with Him. Everywhere we travel we hear churches pleading with God to revive them, their nation, and the world. The widespread dissatisfaction with today's church cannot be solved by best-selling books, church conferences, or an endless stream of Christian trends. When the church seems powerless, only God can make a difference.

As in biblical times, being in God's presence is an awesome, life-changing experience. But because our hearts tend to wander from God, we are often in need of a fresh encounter with Him. We need to be revived. Through salvation, God has granted new life to us through the death and resurrection of Christ. But when we disobey Him, we need His power to renew our relationship once again.

While God is always present in a believer's life, revival is a sacred event when the Holy Spirit draws unmistakably near to His people. Revival involves a fresh encounter with God, and entails a serious, irrevocable accountability. Revival does not call for minor adjustments. It elicits a humble, on-your-face response to our Creator. Revival does not result from an encounter with a doctrine but a response to a Person—God Himself.

In *Fresh Encounter*, you will be taught what the Bible says about God's requirements for fellowship with Him. As you read Scripture, the Holy Spirit will assist you to understand and apply what it says. Instead of merely studying Bible verses; you will encounter the living God, because every encounter with God's Word is a meeting with its Author.

The goal of *Fresh Encounter* begins with seeing Christians and churches revived. A revival can only occur among God's people. But once believers experience a revival, they should work with God to see a spiritual awakening occur in the world. A spiritual awakening occurs when large numbers of people are saved and the culture of a city or community begins to change. Unfortunately, we have not witnessed a spiritual awakening in North America in many generations. But if today's Christians are revived then the Lord can work through them to accomplish the miraculous results of a spiritual awakening.

Our hope is that believers will be so revived because of the truths taught in this study that God can use them to affect a spiritual awakening in their communities, their cities, and the world.

Study Tips

The intent for this material is to help you come face-to-face with holy God and, as a result, to be forever transformed. The Scriptures you will study provide a glimpse into God's heart so you can view sin the way He sees it. God's pattern for revival and spiritual awakening will be laid out as it is found in Scripture. The following are a few ideas to help you maximize your experience as you study.

1. Prepare your heart to receive whatever God reveals to you (Hosea 10:12).

Every truth you encounter has the potential to produce spiritual fruit in your life. If your heart is resistant to God's word, you will struggle with some of the scriptures that are presented. If you have cultivated your heart to be receptive to God's word, your life will be changed.

2. Join with a small group to study this material together.

While God does revive individuals, there is a powerful dynamic that occurs when people seek the Lord together (Malachi 3:16). This material is designed as a group study. You certainly can work through it individually, but there is an added dimension to sharing the experience with others. A Leader's Kit is available with DVDs designed for viewing and discussing in a group setting. The Holy Spirit will speak to you as you hear what God is saying to others. As you sense others' hearts cry to live holy lives that glorify God, you will receive fresh impetus to live your own life in obedience to the Lord.

3. Faithfully do the homework each week.

Your relationship with God is the most important thing in your life. It deserves your time and best effort. Scripture promises you will reap what you sow. Your present walk with God is the result of how you have cultivated it. Be sure you take this opportunity to receive everything God intends for you. Arrange your schedule so you can gain the maximum benefit from the next six weeks of study. Carefully set aside enough time to read each day's material. This study covers some of the most challenging truths in the Christian life. Read them slowly and meditate on them. Don't try and to do five days' reading in one sitting. Let the truths soak into your life throughout the week.

Memorize the Scripture for each week. Each verse has been carefully selected. Having these verses in your mind will help you recall the truths presented as you go about your daily life.

Experience God cleansing and filling you with His Word. Each unit has a list of Scriptures in "Cleansing by washing with water through the Word." Pray through each verse and allow the Holy Spirit to rid your life of anything that is robbing you of what God intends for you. He will take each Scripture and reveal to you how you need to adjust your life in accordance with God's desire.

At the end of each unit you will find a section entitled "Encountering God in Prayer." Meditate on what you have learned and ask the Holy Spirit to identify how you must live your life differently from now on. Use these times to enjoy fellowship with God as He adjusts your life to Himself and His will.

Write down the lessons learned. Take notes in the margins of this book or in a separate journal. At the close of each unit, review what God said to you. You may want to keep a summary of your notes in your Bible where you can be regularly reminded of what God is teaching you. Don't file those notes away until God has completed everything He spoke to you about as you studied this material.

4. Enlist people to pray for you and your group as you go through the study.

Prayer has been a key element to every revival. Be sure others are praying for you as you seek the Lord.

5. Expect God to do a fresh work in your life.

James 4:8 promises that if we draw near to God, He will draw near to us. Since the original version of *Fresh Encounter* (1993) by Henry Blackaby and Claude King much has happened in the Christian community and around the world. This new edition has been significantly revised. It has benefited from Richard Blackaby's work of updating the study to include what we have learned as we have walked with many Christians and churches as they encountered God. God has granted each of us the enormous privilege of traveling around the world and visiting numerous Christians and churches who experienced a fresh touch of the Holy Spirit. We have seen what God can do through one individual or church that is wholly yielded to Him. We believe there are enough Christians and churches in the world today to reach humanity for Christ, if only each Christian and every church would surrender fully to God. For that to happen, a mighty revival must sweep through the churches. That is the focus of much of our ministry today and that is why we wrote *Fresh Encounter.*

We are delighted you have chosen to undertake this study! We have seen these truths challenge people from all around the world and set them free. Our prayer is that you will become keenly aware that God stands before you and invites you to be cleansed from your sin. He wants you to begin a qualitatively deeper and more vibrant walk with Him than you have ever experienced. So let's begin this study together, expecting to hear from God and to experience a profound refreshing of our souls and a deepening of our walk with God.

May we continue to tremble with holy fear when God speaks (Isaiah 66:2), and may we be filled with hope and anticipation for what God is going to do in our day among His people for His glory.

Henry and Richard Blackaby, Claude V. King

For more information on Blackaby Ministries International, please visit *www.blackaby.org.*

For more information about the *Fresh Encounter Group Study Kit* or to download the *Fresh Encounter* teaching videos, please visit *www.lifeway.com/freshencounter.*

Introducing

fresh encounter

Small-Group Discussion Guide

✤ † ✤

Leaders: As you begin this new study, ensure that everyone has a *Fresh Encounter* workbook.

Open in prayer.

As you begin this study, it will be vital to become familiar with the others participants as you learn how God desires to bring about revival in your church. Each week, start your gatherings with prayer. Today, ask if anyone has a specific spiritual need or burden. Keep prayer requests focused on issues of spiritual growth. Ask someone to lead the group in prayer as you embark on this spiritual journey together.

View Introductory Session of the Teaching DVD

Truths to Remember

Scriptures to Read

Quotes to Remember

Actions to Take

If you missed this session, go to *www.lifeway.com/freshencounter* to download this and any other session of *Fresh Encounter.*

Discussion Guide

When you hear the word "revival," what image or definition comes to mind?

After the introductory video from Henry and Richard, do you have a different definition in mind now?

For some, the possibility of encountering God might seem exciting and to others it may seem somewhat improbable. Discuss how you view such a radically personal encounter with God.

Have you ever been involved in a church when a sudden movement of God occurred? Describe the experience to the group.

How would such an experience affect your church today?

Henry described the need to come into this study with an expectancy of what God can do in our lives. Thinking about your walk with God as it is today, what might be the result if you experienced a "fresh encounter" with God?

What would be different?

How would others see a change in your life?

Some of us have participated in discipleship studies in the past. Some studies have a profound effect and others have caused little change in our lives.

What do you hope to learn about God that will deepen your knowledge of Him, increase your love for Him, or bring about a reviving of your church?

Richard said on the video that life is a sum of the choices we make. What choices need to be made by believers today to come into a closer walk with God?

Ask someone to read James 4:8 and discuss the promise made by God.

Henry described the secret that many other believers have found is "an intimate fresh encounter with God." Do you know a believer who obviously has a deep relationship with the Lord? Describe how that person's life is different from other Christians you know.

Invite everyone in the group to finish this sentence: "By the end of this study, I hope that ..."

Use the responses to the sentence as the prayer requests of the group members. Lead a closing prayer by asking God to grant a fresh encounter to each person.

Close in prayer.

UNIT 1: GOD'S PATTERN FOR REVIVAL AND SPIRITUAL AWAKENING

Scripture-Memory Verse

"If My people who are called by My name will humble themselves, and pray and seek My face, and turn from their wicked ways, then I will hear from heaven, and will forgive their sin and heal their land."

2 CHRONICLES 7:14, NKJV

Unit OverUnit Overview

DAY 1: REVIVAL AND SPIRITUAL AWAKENING

DAY 2: GOD'S PATTERN FOR REVIVAL, PART 1

DAY 3: GOD'S PATTERN FOR REVIVAL, PART 2

DAY 4: REVIVAL FOR ALL PEOPLE

DAY 5: WHERE ARE YOU?

Cleansing by Washing with Water Through the Word

THE APOSTLE PAUL DECLARED, *"Christ loved the church and gave Himself for her, to make her holy, cleansing her in the washing of water by the word. He did this to present the church to Himself in splendor, without spot or wrinkle or any such thing, but holy and blameless"* (Ephesians 5:25-27). The Holy Spirit uses Scripture to address the sins in our lives and to make us holy and pure. The Spirit also takes God's promises in Scripture and works them into our lives to make us like Christ. At the beginning of each unit, you will find Scripture verses on which we encourage you to meditate. Throughout the week, return to these verses daily and open your heart to what the Holy Spirit is saying to you about each truth.

Wash Out

Are there actions, behaviors, habits, or sins that need to be cleansed from your life? Your family? Your church? Confess them to God. Resolutely turn away from those activities and surrender your life to God.

Soak In

Are there biblical truths, beliefs, or promises that God wants you to apply to your life? Whenever you see something in Scripture that is not yet fully operative in your life, stop and pray that God will work that truth into your life and into the lives of those around you. Are there behaviors and attitudes that your family or church needs to adopt?

> → **Psalm 24:3-5**
>
> → **Psalm 15:1-5**
>
> → **Micah 6:8**
>
> → **2 Peter 1:3-9**
>
> → **Titus 2:11-14**

Keep the verses above in mind as you work through the Bible studies this week. Use the space below to keep a list of the specific lessons you learn from your studies and how God is applying these lessons to your life.

Experiencing God's power

Spiritual Awakening in Wales

Evan Roberts was deeply concerned about the spiritual condition of Wales, his native land. Roberts began his adult life working at a local coal mine. For 13 years he prayed daily that God would revive the churches of his country. In 1904 Roberts surrendered to God's call on his life and enrolled in a Bible college. Roberts became actively involved in a group of students who regularly met to pray for revival and to promote spiritual renewal in area churches.

At the end of a midweek service, Seth Joshua, an evangelist, closed the meeting by praying, "Lord, bend us." The Holy Spirit drove those simple words into Evan Roberts' heart. Over and over Roberts prayed, "O Lord, bend me!" Roberts sensed God calling him to return to his home church in Loughor to lead the young people in a series of meetings. The pastor would not allow Roberts to address the entire congregation that had gathered for the weekly meeting but announced that anyone who wished to remain afterward could hear what Roberts had to say. On that evening, October 31, 1904, 17 people stayed behind to hear Roberts. His message had four points:

- You must put away any unconfessed sin.
- You must put away any doubtful habit.
- You must promptly obey the Spirit.
- You must publicly confess Christ.[1]

All 17 people pledged to follow these guidelines. The Holy Spirit began to work powerfully in this group. Soon crowds were gathering at the church each evening. God's people began to repent of their sin and renew their relationship with Him. Unbelievers came to the services, and many put their faith in Christ. Roberts and other preachers spread out across Wales to speak in churches and saw revival spread. Within two months 70,000 people had become Christians. Within six months, 100,000 people had been born again and added to the churches.

God's activity among His people exerted a profound impact on the community at large. Taverns were closed for lack of business. The crime rate dropped so dramatically that the police had to find new uses for their time. People repaid delinquent debts and made restitution for thefts and other transgressions. There was even a work slowdown in the coal mines as the pit ponies reportedly could no longer understand the reformed language of the converted coal miners! Soon the world took notice of what God was doing in Wales. Before long, similar revival movements occurred worldwide. It all started when God drew 17 of His people back to Him. Once they returned to God in complete surrender, their community, then their nation, and ultimately the world felt the impact.

†

Day 1 ## Revival and Spiritual Awakening

TWO EXTREMELY IMPORTANT TERMS WE WILL STUDY ARE *revival* AND *spiritual awakening*. Both terms have been defined in many different ways. In the space provided, write your own definitions for both.

Revival:

Spiritual Awakening:

The word *revival* can be understood in a variety of ways. It has been used to describe a series of church meetings held for purposes of evangelism or spiritual renewal. This term can also refer to a renewed interest in something, such as classical music or retro car styles. Sometimes the word *revival* is used to describe a spiritual awakening.

What is biblical revival? The word *revive* consists of two Latin words: *re*, meaning *again*, and *vive*, meaning *to live*. Therefore, *revive* means *to live again or be brought back to life, health, or vitality*. *Revival* may describe a return to spiritual health after a period of decline. Revival is not a creation of life but a return to vigorous life. Bearing that in mind, we will use *revival* to describe what God does to His people as He draws them back into a vibrant relationship with Himself. God revives His people by convicting them of their sin, leading them to repent and return to Him. Then they experience the restoration of their spiritual vitality.

Revive means to live again.

Here is a working definition for this study:
Revival is a divinely initiated work in which God's people pray, repent of their sin, and return to a holy, Spirit-filled, obedient love relationship with God.

Take a moment and identify at least three key words or phrases in the definition above. Beside each phrase, make a note of why it is important in a definition of *revival*.

1.

2.

3.

Write the four bullet points from Evan Roberts message in the opening story on a note card and post it somewhere in your home or office as a daily reminder of remaining pure before God.

1.

2.

3.

4.

What impact would a great revival have on your city?

What Is a Spiritual Awakening?

Spiritual awakening occurs when a large number of people or a high percentage of a population are born again in a relatively short period of time. In Wales 100,000 people were converted in six months, beginning in 1904. During the 1857-58 revival in New York, approximately 1 million people joined the churches in one year out of a national population of 30 million.[2] Spiritual awakening generally grows from a period of revival among God's people. Some common by-products of spiritual awakenings are widespread social reform, a marked decrease in crime and unethical behavior, and improvements in society through the efforts of reinvigorated Christians and churches.

Consider the state of churches today, as well as the condition of your nation. Do you think there is a current need for revival and spiritual awakening? Why or why not?

Which statement would you use to describe society today?

[ ]   Judgment is imminent without revival.
[ ]   Society is desperately wicked.
[ ]   There is still time for things to change.
[ ]   There is no need for revival at this time.
[ ]   God is making significant progress today.
[ ]   The need for revival is greatly overstated today.

God's Invitation to Revival

Revival and spiritual awakening are the Lord's work. God determines the time and way in which He will revive His people. Yet He has also clearly established the terms by which He brings revival and spiritual awakening.

"If My people who are called by My name will humble themselves, and pray and seek My face, and turn from their wicked ways, then I will hear from heaven, and will forgive their sin and heal their land."

2 Chronicles 7:14, NKJV

Read 2 Chronicles 7:14 in the margin. What four things does God require of His people before He will revive them?

1.

2.

3.

4.

When God's people meet His requirements, what three things does God promise to do?

1.

2.

3.

Beside each of the three previous answers, place an *R* beside those that address revival and an *S* beside those that address spiritual awakening.

We pray that you will encounter God in such a way that revival will begin with you.

From our vantage point, we believe churches today are desperately in need of revival. Likewise, countries around the world are in profound need of a spiritual awakening. God has established His terms. However, God's people must believe Him and obey Him. As you study this course, we pray that you will encounter God in such a way that revival will begin with you.

Encountering God in Prayer

Review 2 Chronicles 7:14. Ask God what you must do to meet the requirements so that He will forgive your sin and heal your nation. Which portion of the verse should you focus upon in prayer today? As God brings specific things to your mind, write them down. Passionately pray that God's requirements will soon be met in your life.

Day 2 God's Pattern for Revival, Part 1

Created for a Love Relationship

"I am the LORD, I do not change; Therefore you are not consumed, O sons of Jacob."
Malachi 3:6, NKJV

God created people to experience a love relationship with Him. Tragically, people often reject the Creator's divine invitation by refusing to put their trust in Him. Even those who once enjoyed fellowship with the Lord can choose to turn away from Him.

That is why people need revival. Although we can leave God on our own volition, we cannot return to Him without His help.

God's nature remains constant (Malachi 3:6). He is beyond our human understanding, yet He has promised that those who seek Him will find Him (Jeremiah 29:12-13). Although it is impossible to predict exactly what God will do in light of His absolute sovereignty, patterns and principles are found in the Scriptures and throughout history that help us understand the ways God relates to people. The following is an overview of the seven stages that occur in revival.

A Cycle of Sin and Revival in the Book of Judges

The Book of Judges presents a clear pattern for revival. As you read this biblical account, you will observe the repetitive cycle God's people experienced in their walk with Him:

1. The people followed God.

> *"The people worshiped the LORD throughout Joshua's lifetime and during the lifetimes of the elders who outlived Joshua. They had seen all the LORD's great works He had done for Israel."* Judges 2:7

God did not deliver the Israelites from bondage merely so that they could go and live comfortably in the promised land. Rather, God rescued them so that they would be free to enjoy a special relationship with Him (Exodus 19:4-6). Joshua's generation experienced God's incredible power exercised on their behalf. Joshua was a strong spiritual leader who never wavered in his trust in God. The people he led also chose to trust and follow Joshua's God; as a result, they experienced continual victory.

2. The people forsook the Lord.

> *"The Israelites did what was evil in the LORD's sight. They worshiped the Baals."* Judges 2:11

We cannot live on yesterday's walk with God. Neither our parents' faith or our own earlier relationship with Him can serve us in the present. Every day we must choose to walk with God intimately and obediently. The Israelites had heard their parents speak of God's glorious provision and protection, yet turned their devotion elsewhere. To love anything or anyone more than God is to forsake Him.

What are the things we most often love more than God?

3. God defeated the people through their enemies.

> *"The LORD's anger burned against Israel, and He handed them over to marauders who raided them. He sold them to the enemies around them, so that they could no longer resist their enemies."* Judges 2:14

> *"You will call to Me and come and pray to Me, and I will listen to you. You will seek Me and find Me when you search for Me with all your heart."*
> Jeremiah 29:12-13

> *"You have seen what I did to the Egyptians and how I carried you on eagles' wings and brought you to Me. Now is you will listen to Me and carefully keep My covenant, you will be My own possession out of all the peoples, although all the earth is Mine, and you will be My kingdom of priests and My holy nation. These are the words that you are to say to the Israelites."*
> Exodus 19:4-6

God loves us. He knows our relationship with Him brings life and our rejection of Him causes death. Therefore, when we stray, He brings whatever is necessary to bear on our lives so that we return to Him (Deuteronomy 28:25). He does not allow us to remain comfortable in our sin and rebellion. He removes His hedge of protection from us and allows us to experience the pain and despair that come with alienation from our Creator (Isaiah 5:1-7).

4. The people cried out for help.
> *"They suffered greatly. The LORD was moved to pity whenever they groaned."*
> Judges 2:15,18

While prosperity will not generally motivate God's people to cry out to God, tribulation more often brings us to our knees. Revival begins when people recognize their sin and their hearts return to God. Only when we realize our desperate need for God are we in a position to fully enjoy God's presence in our lives.

5. God had compassion and delivered them.
> *"The LORD raised up judges, who saved them from the power of their marauders. The LORD was moved to pity."* Judges 2:16,18

God is an expert at setting people free. When we cry out to Him, His heart is invariably moved with compassion. Regardless of how many times we reject Him and break our promises to Him, His infinite love compels Him to reach out to and save us.

The previous pattern of obedience, apostasy, discipline, despair, deliverance, and restoration was repeated throughout the Book of Judges. Read Judges 3:7-11 as an illustration of this cycle.

Reading Judges 3:7-11, what impresses you about the way God's people rejected Him and had to be restored through His intervention? How does their pattern compare with the way God's people respond to Him today?

In your own words, write the five stages of the Israelites' departure and return to God, demonstrated in the Book of Judges. Refer to pages 19-20 if needed.

1.

2.

3.

4.

5.

God is an expert at setting people free.

apostasy: an intentional rebellion or departure from one's religious beliefs

"The Israelites did what was evil in the LORD's sight; they forgot the LORD their God. ... The LORD's anger burned against Israel, and He sold them to Cushan-rishathaim king of Aram of the Two Rivers, and the Israelites served him eight years. The Israelites cried out to the LORD. So the LORD raised up Othniel ... as a deliverer to save the Israelites. The Spirit of the LORD was on him, and he judged Israel. Othniel went out to battle, and the handed over Cushan-rishathaim king of Aram to him, so that Othniel overpowered him. Then the land was peaceful for 40 years."
Judges 3:7-11

Seven Phases of Revival

Throughout this material we will present a sevenfold pattern for revival we find in Scripture. Notice that the following pattern begins and ends with God, who works in and through His people to redeem a lost world.

Diagram of Revival

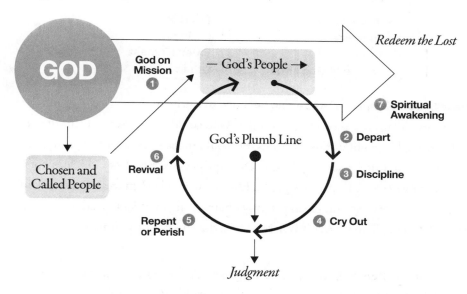

Phase 1: God is on mission to redeem a lost world.

God calls people into a love relationship with Him, and He accomplishes His work through them. God is constantly working to bring people around the world into a saving relationship with Himself (see John 3:16). Once we enter a personal relationship with God, He shares His heart's desire for man's redemption with us and begins to involve us in His mission. As we walk with God, He gives us the desire and the power to serve Him by showing others how they can be saved and serve Him.

God's primary call on our lives is not to activity but to a relationship with Him. We must fight against the confusion of defining Christianity as a set of activities to be performed. God desires for us to act according to our faith, but being a "good person" should be an outworking of our relationship with Him. Only as we walk closely with God can we receive the divine enabling to accomplish what He asks of us.

Have you been tempted to serve God without walking closely with Him? If so, what was the result?

Phase 2: God's people tend to depart from Him, turning to substitutes for His presence, His purposes, and His ways.

The most destructive condition that plagues God's people is their chronic tendency to depart from God. Despite all the heavenly resources and blessings our Lord makes

"God loved the world in this way: He gave His One and Only Son, so that everyone who believes in Him will not perish but have eternal life."
John 3:16

available to us, we inexplicably choose to wander from His protection. We are far too easily enticed by the world's empty promises and shallow temptations. Tragically, we jettison our priceless walk with God for whatever captures our momentary interest.

What are some things in the past that have led you to wander from a close walk with God?

[ ] Work/business   [ ] Addictions
[ ] Selfishness   [ ] Laziness
[ ] Pride   [ ] Entertainment
[ ] Ignorance of God's will   [ ] Other:

Phase 3: God disciplines His people because of His love.

As His people invariably rebel against Him, God could remain serenely indifferent to the inevitable plight of His creatures. He could mock our frail attempts to live independent of Him, knowing the dire consequences we face. But God does not remain unmoved by His people's plight. His love compels Him to actively work in our lives to make the result of sin patently unappealing in order to lead us back to Himself. God will do whatever is necessary to draw us back to Himself.

It is often difficult for us to associate God's discipline with His love. Read Hebrews 12:4-11 and identify whom God disciplines and why.

Whom?

Why?

"You have forgotten the exhortation that addresses you as sons: My son, do not take the Lord's discipline lightly, or faint when you are reproved by Him; for the Lord disciplines the one He loves, and punishes every son whom He receives."
Hebrews 12:5-6

What are some ways God has used to draw you back to Himself when you departed from Him?

[ ] Loss of job/income   [ ] Health problems
[ ] Relationship turmoil   [ ] Emotional pain
[ ] Natural disaster   [ ] Other:

Tomorrow we will examine the final four stages of the revival process.

From the first three stages, which stage do you feel you are in right now?

Now give an example from your life when you have been in one of the other two stages.

Encountering God in Prayer

Reflect on how God led you and worked through your life in the past. Consider times when you clearly knew God was calling you to serve Him in a particular way. Is there any way you have departed from Him and His will for you? Would you be able to say that you are currently in the center of God's will for your life? Take time to pray and make certain that today you are walking with God exactly as you should.

Day 3 God's Pattern for Revival, Part 2

Yesterday we examined the first three phases in God's pattern for revival. Today we will look at the final four phases.

Without looking back, try to list the first three phases of revival.

Phase 1:

Phase 2:

Phase 3:

God eagerly waits for His children to return to Him.

Phase 4: God's people cry out to Him for help.

God's discipline becomes increasingly intense until His people cry out to Him. He is patient and will not force Himself on people or on a church. Like the father of the prodigal son, God eagerly waits for His children to return to Him. He seeks the gentle restoration of His people; but if they will not respond, He increases the intensity of His discipline until they can no longer ignore Him or what He is saying (see Deuteronomy 28:15-68). It takes enormous determination and stubbornness to refuse to repent and return to God after all He does to draw people back to Himself.

But consider the attitudes displayed in the parable of the prodigal son. In Luke 15:17-19, the wayward son prepares himself to beg for his father's mercy. He is ready to be a servant in his father's house rather than live under the disgrace of his new-found poverty. As he approaches his father, he is met with compassion. He is not even able to finish his prepared speech to convince his father to accept him into the household. Read how, the scene plays out in Luke 15:21-23 in the margin.

The father did not desire his son's prepared speech. He only wanted to restore the relationship. We should take heart from Jesus' teaching that when we are prepared to cry out for God's mercy, our Heavenly Father is ready to answer. Our hearts should be ready to seek's God's favor the moment we recognize sin in our lives.

"The son said to him, 'Father, I have sinned against heaven and in your sight. I'm no longer worthy to be called your son.' But the father told his slaves, 'Quick! Bring out the best robe and put it on him; put a ring on his finger and sandals on his feet. Then bring the fattened calf and slaughter it, and let's celebrate with a feast, because this son of mine was dead and is alive again; he was lost and is found!' So they began to celebrate."

Luke 15:21-23

Check all of the reasons you believe people often have to experience hardship before they return to God.

[ ] Stubbornness   [ ] Ignorance of God's ways

[ ] Arrogance and pride   [ ] Selfishness

[ ] Enjoyment of sin's pleasures   [ ] Other:

Phase 5: God calls His people to repent and return to Him or perish.

Repentance is one of the most positive words in Scripture! It means there is hope for fallen sinners. It signifies that change is possible and there is a remedy for sin. God has given no other options for our relationship with Him. Returning to Him is nonnegotiable. Partial, halfhearted, or delayed repentance are all contradictions in terms and unacceptable. Refusing to repent invites negative consequences. Godly repentance, on the other hand, leads to forgiveness and restoration.

Repentance is one of the most positive words in Scripture!

Does the word *repent* normally have a positive or negative connotation for you? Explain why.

Repentance must occur at the heart level. It is not merely changing our behavior outwardly while inwardly we are bitter for being caught in our misadventures in morality. Without returning back to God, He may allow us to suffer under the full consequences of our sin. These consequences could be the breakdown of relationships, illness, or even death. Sin is serious and always carries the ability to destroy our lives.

Phase 6: God revives His repentant people by restoring them to a right relationship with Him.

Revival is God's people returning to Him, their source of life. Repentance returns us not to a system but to a person—God! It also brings forgiveness, freedom, and purity. The ultimate result of repentance is renewed fellowship with God. From this revitalized relationship flow joy and abundant life (see Psalm 51:12).

"Restore the joy of Your salvation to me, and give me a willing spirit."
Psalm 51:12

Why is the experience of God's forgiveness so powerful?

List evidence in your life that you have been restored to a right relationship with God (for example, joy, peace, understanding Scripture)?

Phase 7: God exalts His Son, Jesus, among His people and draws unbelievers to saving faith in Him.

When God's people are rightly related to Him, He displays His glory through their lives to a watching world. Spiritual awakening becomes a natural by-product of a revived people. God receives glory when His people walk closely and obediently with Him. Nonbelievers take notice and are drawn to the God who is being glorified.

Do you find it easy and natural to witness to nonbelievers?   Yes   No

If you answered no, take time to examine your life. List areas of your life in which Jesus is not being glorified through your actions or attitudes. Beside each item you list, write how you plan to change.

List three persons with whom you would like to share the gospel.

1.

2.

3.

God's Purpose for Revival

We should learn to identify the seven phases because of God's purpose in bringing revival to His people. Knowing that we are given to wander from Him, God has prepared for our return. There are two primary reasons revival is critical for believers.

1. God takes delight in our love, and He receives glory from our worship of and obedience to Him. If we have strayed, revival brings us back to walk closely with God so that our lives are pleasing to Him once more.
2. God chooses to accomplish His redemptive purposes through consecrated people. To be useful to Him, we must walk closely with Him.

God is not indifferent to our departure from Him. He will pursue us and do whatever is necessary to bring us back into a loving, obedient relationship with Himself.

What are the two purposes of revival?

1.

2.

God Pursues a Love Relationship

Life's greatest mystery is why God loves His rebellious creation. Why does God continue to reach out to a stubborn, arrogant, foolish people? Why would He pay the ultimate price to obtain redemption for people who were oblivious to what He was doing? Why would the God of heaven care whether His people choose to have fellowship with Him (see Jeremiah 7:13)? But God does care!

Christian history testifies that God's amazing love causes people's hearts to melt in shame and remorse for the calloused way they have responded to His compassion.

" 'Now, because you have done all these things'—this is the LORD's declaration—'and because I have spoken to you time and time again but you wouldn't listen, and I have called to you, but you wouldn't answer.' "
Jeremiah 7:13

David Brainerd, an 18th-century missionary to the American Indians, claimed it was his preaching on God's love that reduced his listeners to tears rather than his sermons on God's judgment.[3] Even a glimpse of God's incredible love for us should drive us to our knees in awe and profound gratitude. Likewise, we should grieve when we realize we have not responded to such love from God.

What thoughts come to your mind as you consider all God has done to reach out to you?

Recall a recent time when you experienced God's forgiveness for one of your failings. Place a check mark beside the word(s) that describe the experience.

[ ] Hope   [ ] Love   [ ] Peace   [ ] Comfort
[ ] Help   [ ] Relief   [ ] Gratitude [ ] Other:

How should a recognition of God's love for us change the way we live?

God Calls People to Join Him in His Work

Besides revitalizing our relationship with the Lord, revival also prepares us to carry out God's will. Throughout history God has brought people into close relationships with Him so that they became useful instruments in His hand to redeem a lost world.

In Christ, God established a new covenant with a new people—the church. This relationship is based on faith, not on keeping the law. Through Peter, God echoed His promise given to the Hebrews long before:

> *"You are a chosen race, a royal priesthood, a holy nation, a people for His possession, so that you may proclaim the praises of the One who called you out of darkness into His marvelous light."* 1 Peter 2:9

Christians are called by God for His pleasure and His purposes. God intends for them to shine the light of Christ in a spiritually dark world. He wants the church to continue what He began with the people of Israel. God continues in His quest to redeem a lost world. Let's look at some ways God uses His church to accomplish His redemptive activity.

We are a chosen generation.

As God's people, we are chosen to be trophies of His amazing grace. We are set apart, not because we deserve it but because we belong to Him. We are not our own but privileged to belong to God's family (see Romans 8:16-17)! As our Father, God deserves and expects our obedience to His purposes to redeem our generation.

Christians are called by God for His pleasure and His purposes.

"The Spirit Himself testifies together with our spirit that we are God's children, and if children, also heirs—heirs of God and co-heirs with Christ—seeing that we suffer with Him so that we may also be glorified with Him."

Romans 8:16-17

We are a royal priesthood.

God did not establish a kingdom with a priesthood—a population ministered to by a few priests who know the secrets of relating to Almighty God. Rather, every believer is a royal priest who enjoys constant access to God. *Royal* implies that each person has a direct relationship with the King and belongs in the royal family. During biblical times the priests equipped God's people to properly worship and serve God. The priest also brought a word from God to the people and represented the people before God. We have the exalted assignment and high privilege to act as God's ambassadors.

We are a holy nation.

The word *holy* means *set apart for God's exclusive use.* We are to be separated from the values and ways of the world. Our outlook on life should be different from unbelievers. We are to reflect God, His character, and His ways. We are commanded to live honorably among unbelievers so they will glorify God (see 1 Peter 2:11-12).

But today's church is not impacting the world for God's kingdom. Just as the Israelites forgot their calling and became entangled in worldly values and pursuits, Christians today are disoriented to what God asks of them. Churches continue holding services, building larger buildings, and launching new programs; but the world becomes increasingly dark and hostile to God. We desperately need reviving.

> **How does the perspective of your identity as a "royal priest" change the way you relate to other believers?**

> **Many unbelievers today say they have rejected the claims of Christianity because of the way Christians live their lives. What are some ways God's people repel unbelievers from God instead of drawing them to Him?**

God is on mission to redeem a lost world. He could use any method but has chosen to work through a people consecrated to Himself. When God's people turn away from their covenant relationship with Christ, they are no longer prepared to serve God and bring Him glory. God disciplines them to draw them back to Himself. Once God's people repent and return to Him, He forgives them and uses them once again to accomplish His purposes. God takes our relationship with Him extremely seriously because it gives our lives meaning and purpose as we relate to Him and serve Him.

Encountering God in Prayer

Take a moment to reflect on what kind of priest you have been for God. Have you been faithful, always prepared to follow His leadership? Have you been royal, reflecting the King you serve? Have you been holy, keeping yourself untainted by the world so that you could be a consecrated instrument in God's hand? If you have not, pray and ask God to consecrate you afresh for his service. If you have been serving God faithfully, ask God to take your consecration and your service to a deeper level.

Day 4 Revival for All People

The Shantung Revival

In the 1920s Christian missionaries in north China were grieved over the lethargic condition of their churches. Members showed little interest for spiritual concerns. They began to wonder if many of the people in the churches had accepted Christianity intellectually but had never been spiritually born again. They began to devote one day a month to praying together for revival.

In March 1927 the Chinese Southern Revolutionary Army burned Nanking, and missionaries were ordered to Chefoo for possible evacuation. While the missionaries were together, waiting to learn whether they could continue their work, they began to study the Scriptures and ask the Lord why they had been removed from their field.

Some of the displaced missionaries asked Marie Monsen, an evangelical Lutheran missionary from Norway, to join their prayer meetings. God used her to challenge them to get right with Him. The group spent days before God confessing every known sin. They were reconciled with one another as God drew His people back to Himself. Marie asked the missionaries three penetrating questions:

1. Have you been born of the Spirit?
2. What evidence do you have of the new birth?
3. Have you been filled with the Holy Spirit?[4]

What are your answers to Marie Monsen's three questions?

1.

2.

3.

plumb line: a cord with a lead weight at the end to determine a straight perpendicular line

The hunger for spiritual vitality caused the missionaries to do much soul-searching. One missionary, observed, "We felt an electric excitement, a feeling that God was preparing us for something we had never known before."[5] Once God's people drew close to Him, He used them to powerfully impact China for Christ.

God set His plumb line against the lives of the Chinese church leaders, and they saw how short they fell of His expectations. An evangelist for 25 years, Mr. Chow, realized he was trusting in his good works for salvation but not in Christ. He gave his life to Christ and henceforth refused to be paid for his preaching.[6] Lucy Wright, a missionary nurse for 9 years, realized she had only joined the church but had not been born again. She turned her life over to Christ for the first time.[7] By 1932 thousands of people in China were coming to Christ. One example was a school where six hundred girls and nine hundred of one thousand boys professed faith in Christ in 10 days.

Revival produces exponential results. New converts went everywhere telling people what Jesus had done for them. Those who turned to Christ took down their "house gods" and burned them. The hearts of God's people were full of praise and thanksgiving. Joyful singing filled the services. New hymns were written, and Scriptures were put to music. Believers developed an insatiable hunger for God's Word. Classes met nightly to study the Bible. Enrollment in Bible schools and seminaries dramatically increased. Spiritually stagnant churches were reinvigorated. Church attendance multiplied, and members enthusiastically participated in worship, prayer, and discipleship. Prayer meetings lasted two or three hours as people were reconciled with God and prayed for unbelievers. Broken families and relationships were healed.[8] Once God's people realized how far they had drifted from Him, they enthusiastically returned, and soon vast regions of China felt the impact.

Marie Monsen asked three simple questions. Why did they have such a dramatic impact on the missionaries and churches in China?

List some of the ways revival impacted churches in China during the Shantung Revival.

Once people have their relationships with God made right, their other relationships are inevitably affected.

The Shantung Revival affected people in China in a variety of ways. From the saving of the lost to the mending of families to the reinvigorating of stagnant churches—God impacted China. When God brings revival, every human relationship can be restored to the way God intends. Once people have their relationships with God made right, their other relationships are inevitably affected.

Revival Impacts Individuals

God intends for individuals to enjoy close communion with Him. When people like Joseph, Elijah, David, Mary, Peter, or Paul walked closely with God, they not only experienced God's joy, peace, and power but also witnessed God doing amazing things in and through their lives. One individual, no matter how ordinary, who is totally surrendered and consecrated to God, can become a powerful instrument in His hand.

Sin, however, impairs our fellowship with God and hampers our effectiveness in doing His work. Out of His grace, God chose to walk with David and bless him. Ultimately, God raised the lowly shepherd boy to become a king and a great blessing

One individual, no matter how ordinary, who is totally surrendered and consecrated to God, can become a powerful instrument in His hand.

to his people. Then David grievously sinned against God and against Uriah. This is how David described the consequence of his sin:

> "*When I kept silent, my bones became brittle*
> *from my groaning all day long.*
> *For day and night Your hand was heavy on me;*
> *my strength was drained as in the summer's heat.*"
> Psalm 32:3-4

Read Psalm 51:11-12 in the margin. When David repented of his sin, God forgave him and restored His presence and joy in David's life.

How did David feel when he was estranged from God because of his sin?

What feelings have you experienced when you held on to your sin?

Revival Impacts Families

God designed the family to be a source of joy, peace, refuge, and safety. In the context of family, a husband and a wife can experience a loving, trusting relationship (see Genesis 2:24-25). When God called Abraham, He promised to use his family to be a blessing to all the families of the earth (see Genesis 12:3). The family is the primary setting where God wants children to be taught about Him (see Deuteronomy 6:6-9). God's truths and promises are to be passed down from one generation to the next (see Isaiah 59:21).

However, sin erects barriers between husbands and wives (see Genesis 3:7). Sin leads to anger, even murder (see Genesis 4:8). It causes adultery and divorce between spouses and estrangement between children and parents (see Matthew 19:3-9). When God brings revival, marriages are restored and broken families are mended. Only God can soften the hearts of spouses, parents, and children (see Malachi 4:6). He can empower them to forgive one another and equip them to love as Christ loves.

What do you think would happen to your family if God brought revival?

Revival Impacts Churches

Christ is the head of the church (see Colossians 1:18) and is the one who builds the church (see Matthew 16:18). God adds people to the body as it pleases Him so that members are interdependent with one another (see 1 Corinthians 12:12-31). God intends for congregations to be united in caring for one another and in boldly sharing their faith (see Acts 4:31-33).

Why do churches dwindle and die? They lose sight of their purpose and neglect their relationship with the head of their church. Sin causes division among members. Churches can become so focused on gaining numbers, collecting offerings, or building buildings that they forget that Christ should receive glory from all the churches do. Congregations can become like the church at Laodicea, which claimed, "I'm rich; I have become wealthy, and need nothing." Yet this church did not realize that God saw them as "wretched, pitiful, poor, blind, and naked" (Revelation 3:17). Just as sin binds individuals and families, it deceives and destroys congregations.

When the church in Ephesus needed revival, the risen Christ cautioned: "Remember then how far you have fallen; repent and do the works you did at first. Otherwise I will come to you and remove your lampstand from its place—unless you repent" (Revelation 2:5).

Just as sin binds individuals and families, it deceives and destroys congregations.

Why was repentance so important as the first step for the church at Ephesus?

What are some reasons churches get off track from what God originally called them to do?

What might it take for churches to return to God's plan for them?

Revival Impacts Nations

Read 2 Chronicles 7:14 (NKJV) again to see what it says about reviving nations:
"If My people who are called by My name will humble themselves, and pray and seek My face, and turn from their wicked ways, then I will hear from heaven, and will forgive their sin and heal their land."

How would you describe the spiritual and moral condition of your nation today? Circle all that apply:

Healthy	Desperately sick	Experiencing God's judgment
Deceived	Needs reform	Continually becoming more depraved
Blind	Beyond hope	Experiencing revival
Apathetic	Close to judgment	

Did you notice what God said must happen before the land would be healed? He did not say, "When the media experience positive changes" or "When government is reformed." God did not even say, "When Christians pray for their nation to be revived." The Lord made it clear that the nation would be healed when *God's people* repented of their sin. The reason nations need revival is that God's people have not been the salt and light God intended for them to be (see Matthew 5:13-16). When

Christians see how wicked their nation is becoming, it is not the time to point a condemning finger at unbelievers. Rather, it ought to break Christians' hearts that their presence is not making a more significant difference in their land. It should not be surprising when unbelievers behave according to their nature. It is tragic when Christians do not act according to theirs.

It should not be surprising when unbelievers behave according to their nature. It is tragic when Christians do not act according to theirs.

> **In what ways should the church have a strong spiritual impact on the nation?**

> **Why do unbelievers often exert a more powerful influence over a nation than believers do?**

Revival is a return to the life God originally provided. For individual Christians, it brings them back to the state of enthusiastic obedience to their Lord they had when they first became followers of Christ. Revival returns the spiritual life and vitality they once enjoyed before sin robbed them of it. For families, it is returning to God's intention when He first fashioned them into families. It involves restoration, forgiveness, and reestablishing a pure commitment to follow Christ. For churches, it is a return to God's purpose when He first assembled the congregation. It involves corporate repentance by His people. Finally, national revival happens when God's people return to Him and unbelievers feel the impact of God's presence and work. Tomorrow we will examine the symptoms of a person or group's need for revival.

Revival is a return to the life God originally provided.

Encountering God in Prayer

Take time to examine your Christian walk. If you've kept a journal, review your spiritual journey. Are you as close to God now as you have ever been? Are your marriage and family fulfilling every purpose God has for them? Is Christ being glorified in your church? Is your nation conducting itself in such a way that God would be pleased to bless it? If not, spend time in prayer, asking God to show you in what ways you and others must return to God.

Day 5 Where Are You?

Revival in Korea

According to Jonathan Goforth, the Korean revival of 1907 began when the Central Presbyterian Church held an eight-day series of meetings for universal prayer. Many of its members sensed that God was about to renew the church, yet each meeting concluded in the normal fashion. As the final service drew to a close, Elder Keel suddenly rose to his feet. People were startled when this greatly respected church leader confessed, "I am an Achan."[8] (See Joshua 7.) He tearfully admitted that a year earlier he had managed the financial affairs of a deceased friend's widow. In the process he stole some of the estate's money. He admitted his sin, vowed to make immediate restitution, and acknowledged that his sin was hindering the Spirit's work in their church. Immediately, a powerful conviction of sin swept over the congregation, and people lined up to confess their sins. Revival burst forth.

Keel had faithfully served the Lord for years and was highly respected by his congregation. But he had fallen. Sin had crept into his life through what he perceived to be a small act. No one had discovered his dishonesty, yet he knew his spiritual vitality had waned. He was a faithful church member, but he lacked God's blessing until he confessed his sin. Then the Holy Spirit immediately convicted many others in the church that they had allowed sin into their lives and were no longer experiencing God's power. Revival came to the church and then spread out to the nation when one man was willing to confess and repent of his sin.

God Used an Ordinary Businessperson

When God approached Abraham, it was not merely to have fellowship with Him. God intended to use Abraham's life to bless generations to come. The Bible tells us that God invited Abraham to become involved in accomplishing His purposes.

Look up and read Genesis 12:1-3; 17:1,7-9. Answer the following questions.

Who is the focus of these Scriptures—God or Abraham?

In Genesis 17:1 how was Abraham to walk before God?

Describe the effect God's covenant with Abraham was to have on Abraham's children.

In calling Abraham, God was setting His plan in motion to redeem an entire world. God told Abraham to follow Him, to be blameless, and to teach his children to follow God. God kept His promises and built Abraham's descendants into a nation. Ultimately, the Lord brought salvation to all humanity through one of Abraham's descendants—Christ.

Throughout history God has called people to Himself so that He had a holy people through whom to work. When God delivered the Israelites from slavery in Egypt, it was not so that they could become wealthy and comfortable in the promised land. Read the call God gave His people in Exodus 19:3-6 (in the margin).

Achan: an Israelite who disobeyed God and brought judgment upon all of Israel in Joshua 7

Revival came to the church and then spread out to the nation when one man was willing to confess and repent of his sin.

"Moses went up the mountain to God, and the LORD called to him from the mountain: 'This is what you must say to ... the Israelites: You have seen what I did to the Egyptians and how I carried you on eagles' wings and brought you to Me. Now if you will listen to Me and carefully keep My covenant, you will be My own possession out of all the peoples ... and you will be My kingdom of priests and My holy nation.'"
Exodus 19:3-6

We know God brought the Israelite people to a land of prosperity, but more importantly, God said, "I ... brought you to Me." God's plan for Israel was not primarily a place but a relationship. That is what made them unique from any other people. From their relationship with God, the Israelites would be God's special messengers of salvation to the entire world.

Who have been the ordinary people God has used to express His love and message of salvation to you?

See if you can list, from memory, the seven phases of revival. If you can't remember them all, look back at the diagram on page 21.

1.

2.

3.

4.

5.

6.

7.

Now put a check mark beside the stage that best describes your present spiritual condition.

The phases of revival are cyclical. We begin by walking closely, excitedly, and obediently with Christ. But then sin lures our trust away from God and toward substitutes. Even as we turn away from God, He relentlessly pursues us and attempts to draw us back to Himself. God said to His people, through His prophet Jeremiah:

> *"'I did give them this command: Obey Me, and then I will be your God, and you will be My people. You must walk in every way I command you so that it may go well with you.' Yet they didn't listen or pay attention but walked according to their own advice and according to their own stubborn, evil heart. They went backward and not forward. Since the day your ancestors came out of the land of Egypt until this day, I have sent all My servants the prophets to you time and time again."* Jeremiah 7:23-25

What does this Scripture indicate about God?

What does this Scripture indicate about God's people?

When people do not respond to God's loving appeals, He disciplines them. God has numerous ways to reprimand His people. He can allow defeat in our lives or disasters. He can afflict our health or remove our prosperity. Because God is sovereign over nature, He can use it to gain His people's attention. God's intent is to make any substitute for God so undesirable that we return to Him. When our discomfort becomes unbearable, we repent and cry out to God for deliverance. Then God forgives and delivers by restoring us to a healthy relationship with Himself. Afterward we are in a place to be useful to Him in accomplishing His divine purposes. Unfortunately, it often does not take long before we allow sin to reenter our lives as the cycle of rebellion and return repeats itself.

As you continue in this study, keep in mind that this is not merely a picture of the way ancient people walked with God. A study of revival is more relevant than reading this morning's newspaper. People need revival today as much as they did two thousand years ago. It is our prayer that your heart will be sensitive to all that the Holy Spirit will say to you through this study. Though you may have begun this study with a concern for your children or church or nation, revival always begins with you.

A study of revival is more relevant than reading this morning's newspaper.

Once we are rightly related to God, He works through us to accomplish His redemptive purposes for our family and church and nation. If you decided to undertake this study so that you could understand how God might revive others, you have missed the point. Revival begins with us. So open your heart and mind to all God wants to do in your life and then watch and see how God uses your submissive life to draw others to Himself.

Encountering God in Prayer

Turn to page 21 and look at the diagram of the seven phases of revival. Identify where your life presently lines up. Ask yourself, *Where would God see my life right now?* Prayerfully ask the Lord how your life has come to be where it is spiritually. Was there a particular sin you allowed into your life? Have you disobeyed Him? What must you do to return to a healthy, vibrant walk with God once again? Do it today.

1. Malcom McDow and Alvin Reid, *Firefall: How God Has Shaped History Through Revivals* (Nashville: B&H Publishing Group, 1997), 278.
2. Arthur Strickland, *The Great American Revival* (Cincinnati, OH: Standard Press, 1934), 16.
3. Jonathan Edwards, *The Works of Jonathan Edwards* (Pennsylvania: The Banner of Truth Trust, 1834), 2:353.
4. Bertha Smith, *Go Home and Tell* (Nashville: B&H Publishing Group, 1995), 43.
5. C. L. Culpepper, *The Shantung Revival* (n.p., n.d.), 9.
6. Smith, *Go Home and Tell*, 44–45.
7. Ibid., 48–50.
8. Adapted from Culpepper, *The Shantung Revival*, and Smith, *Go Home and Tell*. See these books for more information.
9. Jonathan Goforth, *When the Spirit's Fire Swept Korea* (Grand Rapids: Zondervan Publishing House, 1958), 8.

Small-Group Discussion Guide

Open in prayer.

Ahead of time, ask someone to be prepared to pray. Invite prayer requests and ask the group for prayer requests that pertain to personal and corporate revival. Listen for how God is presently working in their lives through the study so that the group will know how to pray for them. Once people have had an opportunity to share, call on the person appointed to pray.

Before you began this week's study, what were your views of revival and spiritual awakening? Has your perspective changed in any way after the first week?

What was most intriguing, challenging, or offensive as you began this study on revival?

View Session 1 of the Teaching DVD

Truths to Remember

Scriptures to Read

Quotes to Remember

Actions to Take

If you missed this session, go to www.lifeway.com/freshencounter to download this and any other session of Fresh Encounter.

Discussion Guide

In the introduction to our homework, the story of Evan Roberts and Seth Joshua was told. Remember that Evan Roberts asked the people who stayed after the service to pray about four issues. They were:

- *You must put away any unconfessed sin.*
- *You must put away any doubtful habit.*
- *You must promptly obey the Spirit.*
- *You must publicly confess Christ.*

What is your personal reaction to being confronted by these issues?

Read 2 Chronicles 7:14. What are God's people called upon to do when seeking God's reviving power?

Discuss the seven stages of revival from the diagram on page 21. What stage do you feel is the most common one for churches to be in today?

Discuss the Blackabys' definition of revival: "*Revival is a divinely initiated work in which God's people pray, repent of their sin, and return to a holy, Spirit-filled, obedient love relationship with God.*"

Why do God's people struggle to be faithful to our God who loves us so deeply?

What are some reasons for which churches tend to depart from God?

Invite people to share an experience they have had with one of the seven phases of revival. You don't need to evaluate or correct their sharing. Just ask questions to help clarify what they experienced.

Read 1 Peter 2:9 and discuss God's calling on the lives of believers. How will understanding our calling reorient a Christian to live in a closer relationship to Christ?

In day 3 you listed persons with whom you would like to share the gospel. Ask a volunteer to give the first name of someone on their list and to pray for that person.

Day 4 discussed how revival can come to all levels of human interaction, beginning with the individual and extending to an entire nation.

Which of the four categories—individual, family, church, or nation—most intrigues you? Why?

How would our community and city operate differently if revival came to our church?

Invite people to share, in light of the first week's study, what they sense God may want to do in their lives, their families, their church, and their nation.

Close in prayer.

UNIT 2: GOD'S PEOPLE TEND TO DEPART FROM HIM

Scripture-Memory Verses

"Watch out, brothers, so that there won't be in any of you an evil, unbelieving heart that departs from the living God. But encourage each other daily, while it is still called today, so that none of you is hardened by sin's deception."

Hebrews 3:12-13

Unit Overview

Cleansing by Washing with Water Through the Word

THIS WEEK WE WILL COME FACE-TO-FACE WITH OURSELVES. To take a survey of our own heart can be a difficult—even painful—journey. But we can discover a renewed relationship with Christ and a deeper appreciation of God's care for us. Remember Paul's words from Ephesians 5:25-27: *"Christ loved the church and gave Himself for her, to make her holy, cleansing her in the washing of water by the word. He did this to present the church to Himself in splendor, without spot or wrinkle or any such thing, but holy and blameless."*

Continue to keep your heart open to what the Holy Spirit is saying to you through the following Scriptures and the truths He teaches.

Wash Out

Are there actions, behaviors, habits, or sins that need to be washed out of your life? Your family? Your church? Confess them and turn away from them and to God.

Soak In

Are there good things God wants to soak into your life? Your family? Your church? Pray that God will work each of these into your life and will help you become all He desires for you to be.

- → **Romans 12:1-2**
- → **Matthew 5:21-24**
- → **Matthew 5:27-28**
- → **Matthew 5:31-32**
- → **Matthew 5:33-34,37**
- → **Psalm 1:1-2**
- → **2 Timothy 3:1-5**
- → **Titus 3:9-10**

Keep the verses above in mind as you work through the Bible studies this week. Use the space below to keep a list of the specific lessons you learn from your studies and how God is applying these lessons to your life.

Experiencing God's power

Revival in Northampton

In December 1734 a revival occurred in the Northampton congregation, led by its 31-year-old pastor, Jonathan Edwards. The young people in the congregation were the cause of concern among the adults because they were embracing many worldly pleasures. However, the sudden deaths of two young adults prompted many other young adults to spontaneously turn to God. Soon the older members of the church were also experiencing revival. In December 1734 a young woman who was known to be one of the town's most notorious sinners became a follower of Christ. Her dramatic life transformation clearly displayed the miraculous work of God's grace. By early 1735 the church was filled to capacity. Within six months 300 people had been converted, though the town's population was only 1,100. Edwards said, "God has also seemed to have gone out of his usual way in the quickness of his work, and the swift progress his Spirit has made in his operation, on the hearts of many."[1] "There was scarcely a single person in the town, either old or young, that was left unconcerned about the great things of the eternal world. ... Our public assemblies were then beautiful; the congregation was alive in God's service, every one earnestly intent on the public worship. ... Our public praises were then greatly enlivened; God was then served ... in the beauty of holiness."[2]

As America was swept up in a Great Awakening during the following years, Edwards befriended many of the revival leaders, such as George Whitefield. During this exhilarating period, Edwards penned his thoughts and observations, which became some of history's most influential writings on spiritual awakening. Nevertheless, the revival fires eventually died out. Then in 1740 revival swept over Edwards's congregation once again, and people returned to vibrant relationships with God. Eventually, that tide of revival receded. On the heels of revival, a faction developed within Edwards's church, fueled by disgruntled members. In 1750 this group succeeded in dismissing Edwards as pastor, though he was a godly man at the center of God's unmistakable activity. Here was a congregation at the epicenter of a great awakening, yet some church members were disoriented to God to the point of ousting their pastor and quenching the Holy Spirit's work.

✠ † ✠

Day 1 Wayward Hearts

Deceived

Once after Henry preached about authentic Christianity, a man came during the decision time and tearfully confessed he had never truly surrendered his life to Christ and established a personal relationship with God. Although he was a long-time church member and served as a deacon and Sunday School teacher, he was not a child of God. For years he assumed that his church service and religious lifestyle meant he was a Christian. But that day, confronted with a biblical description of genuine Christianity, this man could be deceived no longer.

The key to the Christian experience is the heart. God offers the same marvelous invitation to each person to know Him and to enjoy fellowship with Him. Yet the condition of our heart determines the quality of our walk with God. The prophet declared that,

> *"The heart is more deceitful than anything else and desperately sick—who can understand it?"* Jeremiah 17:9

Your heart can be right with God one day and distant from Him the next. You can be receptive to God's Word one day and resistant to it the next. That was the problem with the people in Northampton during Jonathan Edwards's time. Despite experiencing profound seasons of revival, they became distracted from following God.

Turn back to the account of revival in Northampton under Jonathan Edwards's leadership (see p. 41). Underline the various positive outcomes of the Northampton revivals.

Using a different-colored pen, underline the negative things that occurred in Northampton. Notice how both good and evil occurred among the same people.

What do you think are some of the reasons people who have experienced God powerfully working in their lives would turn away from Him?

Following God

It is perplexing that we can choose to turn our backs on our Heavenly Father despite all He has done for us. God created us to enjoy a love relationship with Him. He invites us to join Him in His worldwide redemptive work. He is not a distant Creator but a loving, personal God. His expectations of us are neither mysterious nor impossible to understand and follow.

"This command that I give you today is certainly not too difficult or beyond your reach. It is not in heaven, so that you have to ask, 'Who will go up to heaven, get it for us, and proclaim it to us so that we may follow it?' And it is not across the sea, so that you have to ask, 'Who will cross the sea, get it for us, and proclaim it to us so that we may follow it?' But the message is very near you, in your mouth and in your heart, so that you may follow it. See, today I have set before you life and prosperity, death and adversity. For I am commanding you today to love the Lord your God, to walk in His ways, and to keep His command, statutes, and ordinances, so that you may live and multiply, and the Lord your God may bless you in the land you are entering to possess."

Deuteronomy 30:11-16

Read Deuteronomy 30:11-16 in the margin on the previous page.

In your own words, what does the passage declare about God's Word?

What does God ask His people to do in order to experience life?

God asks us to do three things: (1) love Him, (2) walk in His ways, and (3) keep His commands. More than anything else, God desires our love. His ways are contrary to our own self-destructive inclinations, and they go against the world's dangerous temptations (see Isaiah 55:8-9). Yet even though God's ways are vastly different from our ways, His will is not obscure or nebulous, requiring us to consult a religious guru to understand it. The Holy Spirit is present within Christians to guide and empower us in every act of obedience (see Galatians 5:16,25). God has done everything necessary to enable us to obey Him, follow Him, and participate with Him in His redemptive mission.

Place a check mark beside some of the reasons that have caused your heart to grow cold toward God in the past.

[ ] **Distracted by job**   [ ] **Spiritual laziness**
[ ] **Poor relationship with spouse**   [ ] **Habitual sins**
[ ] **Overload of religious activities** [ ] **Grief**
[ ] **Lack of prayer and Bible study**   [ ] **Difficult times in life**
[ ] **Other:**

Shifting Hearts

God "has blessed us with every spiritual blessing" (Ephesians 1:3), and "His divine power has given us everything required for life and godliness" (2 Peter 1:3). God has done amazing things for us, yet we continue to leave Him. How does this happen? How do we grow disoriented to God? God explains that it is a matter of divided attention: "If your heart turns away and you do not listen and you are led astray to bow down to other gods and worship them ..." (Deuteronomy 30:17).

Apostasy often begins as a distraction when our focus is diverted from God to circumstances, people, or worldly enticements. People seldom realize it is happening until they have drifted away from Him. It originates with a change of heart, and then separation in the relationship occurs. The alienation from God follows a downward course as people struggle to obey Him. They make ungodly choices and rationalize their neglect to follow God. They grow comfortable in their worldly living so that their hearts are cold to the Holy Spirit's call to return. Eventually, they turn to substitutes for God. Idols do not condemn their sin or convict them of their ungodly behavior. Surrogates do not hold them accountable or ask them to do things they

"'My thoughts are not your thoughts, and your ways are not My ways.' This is the LORD's declaration. 'For as heaven is higher than earth, so My ways are higher than your ways, and My thoughts than your thoughts.'"
Isaiah 55:8-9

"I say then, walk by the Spirit and you will not carry out the desire of the flesh. If we live by the Spirit, we must also follow the Spirit."
Galatians 5:16,25

do not want to do. Eventually, like the Israelites of old, they "bow down to other gods and worship them" (Deuteronomy 30:17). This is how a person, family, church, denomination, or nation departs from God.

In your own words, describe how people depart from a loving relationship with God to trust in idols of the heart.

On the continuum below, place a mark where your life presently is in relation to God.

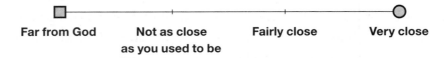

| Far from God | Not as close as you used to be | Fairly close | Very close |

God knows our heart's condition. He knew His people would be habitually tempted to depart from Him, so He issued this solemn warning:

> *"If your heart turns away ... I tell you today that you will certainly perish and you will not live long. ... I call heaven and earth as witnesses against you today that I have set before you life and death, blessing and curse. Choose life so that you and your descendants may live, love the LORD your God, obey Him, and remain faithful to Him. For He is your life."*
> Deuteronomy 30:17-20

Underline the consequences God mentioned in the previous passage for those whose hearts turn away from Him.

The reason we need revival is that our hearts are constantly being drawn away from God. Following God is not difficult if our hearts are set on doing so. Therefore, when we seek revival, it is inadequate merely to try to reform our behavior. We must allow God to thoroughly deal with our hearts. That is the only way to address any attitudes, affections, and loyalties which are drawn away from Christ. Revival is essentially a restoration of our hearts.

Revival is essentially a restoration of our hearts.

Encountering God in Prayer

Look back at the continuum depicting your walk with God. Prayerfully ask the Lord where He wants your walk with Him to be. Revival is not about our wishes but God's leadership. Ask Him to show you where your heart has departed from Him and what must change for you to have the close walk with Him that He desires. Commit yourself to pay any price, to make any adjustment, and to renounce any sin in order to have the walk with God He is inviting you to experience.

Day 2 Cracked Cisterns

A Foolish Bargain

A Christian man was faithfully serving the Lord. He taught a large weekly Bible study at his church. He was active in a Christian men's ministry. He went on mission trips. He had a loving family and a successful career. Then he began to wonder whether he was somehow missing out on what life had for him. He started cutting corners in his business to maximize profits. He began embellishing the truth to his clients. He started viewing his marriage as a restriction. Compromises became habitual for him, and eventually, he left his wife and children. The business started to crumble as his dishonesty began to catch up with him. He told new lies to cover his old lies. His health suffered. His children began to struggle. His personal relationships were in shambles. Eventually, he committed a crime and ended up in jail. To the very end, he proclaimed his innocence and maintained that his walk with God had never been better. Such a dramatic downfall seemed incomprehensible. But it happened one decision at a time as the man listened to the counsel of his deceptive heart.

Such a dramatic downfall seemed incomprehensible.

Every day people choose, whether or not they realize it, to trade what is precious for something that is worthless. Despite God's amazing invitation to walk in intimate, vibrant, victorious fellowship with Him, His people inevitably forsake Him, enticed by transitory, cheap substitutes. Read about the Israelites' departure and listen to the cry of God's heart as He described how His people callously forsook Him:

> *"What fault did your fathers find in Me*
> *that they went so far from Me,*
> *followed worthless idols,*
> *and became worthless themselves?*
> *They stopped asking: Where is the LORD? …*
> *I brought you to a fertile land*
> *to eat its fruit and bounty,*
> *but after you entered, you defiled My land;*
> *you made My inheritance detestable.*
> *The priests quit asking, Where is the LORD?'*
> *The experts in the law no longer knew Me,*
> *and the rulers rebelled against Me.*
> *The prophets prophesied by Baal*
> *and followed useless idols.*
> *Therefore, I will bring a case against you again.*
> *This is the LORD's declaration. …*
> *See if there has ever been anything like this:*
> *Has a nation ever exchanged its gods?*
> *(but they were not gods!)*
> *Yet My people have exchanged their Glory*

for useless idols.
Be horrified at this, heavens;
be shocked and utterly appalled,"
    This is the LORD's declaration.
For My people have committed a double evil:
They have abandoned Me,
the fountain of living water,
and dug cisterns for themselves,
cracked cisterns that cannot hold water."
Jeremiah 2:5-13

God painted a graphic picture of the inevitable consequences when people forsake their love relationship with Him to pursue fleeting, worldly enticements. In Jeremiah 2 God described a parched desert with hot, withering, sandy winds. But in the midst of the desolate wilderness flows a bubbling, deep spring delivering an endless supply of refreshing water. In Scripture God is often likened to life-giving water, for He alone is able to endow people with life as He fills them with Himself. The Bible says, "The LORD your God ... is your life" (Deuteronomy 30:20). Jesus said, "I am ... the life" (John 14:6) and referred to Himself as Living Water (see John 4:14).

A cistern is a reservoir for storing water—not a source capable of producing fresh water. A broken cistern is totally useless. The biblical metaphor demonstrates the colossal folly of rejecting a fresh, cool, endless supply of spring water in favor of a broken, empty, man-made container. Incredibly, Christians continue to reject the living water of Christ to seek surrogate, worldly gods that cannot satisfy. The twofold tragedy is that not only do we reject our loving Heavenly Father, but the artificial substitutes we embrace, though they may offer illusory comfort and pleasure, also fail to deliver the very thing we seek—abundant life.

cistern: a man-made reservoir for storing water

Place the following items under the appropriate columns:
The Holy Spirit's guidance; God's peace; Trusting in friends; God's provision; Corporate success; God's power; Lust; Material possessions; Fellowship with God; People's approval; Anger
   Broken Cisterns   *Living Water*

Examine the two lists and answer this question: Why would people choose imperfect substitutes when they could enjoy the abundant life God provides?

List any broken cisterns that have distracted you from your relationship with God. Beside each write what you should do about them.

The world is filled with enticing advertisements and temptations that promise limitless joy. For those who succumb to the lure of worldly attractions, it never takes long to experience disappointment and disillusionment. Then the only wise thing to do is to reject the broken cisterns we have foolishly trusted in and return to the Lord in the same manner as the prodigal son (see Luke 15:11-32).

Encountering God in Prayer

As ludicrous as it seems that a thirsty person in a desert would pass up spring water for an empty, dry cistern, we make the same misguided trade ourselves. Spend some quiet time before the Lord and ask the Holy Spirit to bring to mind any broken cisterns in your life. Make a list of the things in your past that you have used as substitutes for finding fulfillment in your life. Consider how God feels about your rejection of Him. Ask the Lord to show you how to return to Him.

Day 3 Idols of the Heart

In Whom Do You Trust?

A Christian college professor seemed to have a great career. He was active in his church but did not attend the church prayer meeting. He enjoyed a comfortable income and took pride in his boldness for expressing his convictions. But difficulty arose with the head of his college department, and he was told he would lose his job. Devastated, the professor began to attend the weekly prayer meeting and share his personal struggles with his church family. They prayed for him and encouraged him as he appealed the decision by the college department. He won his appeal. The professor had discovered and lived out a deeper faith than ever before.

However, the department head appealed the ruling. This time, in preparation for the final hearing, the professor did not leave his destiny in God's hands but instead hired a well-known attorney. The fulfilling relationship he discovered with Christ began to wane. He stopped attending the prayer meetings as he and his attorney feverishly prepared a defense. Advised by his attorney, he stopped sharing his prayer requests with his church family. The attorney prepared a seemingly foolproof case, so it came as a shock when he lost his case and was dismissed from his job. Many Christians claim to trust in God, but their actions prove they rely on worldly methods and resources to receive things God promised to provide Himself.

How did the man in the story above depart from the belief that God is trustworthy?

Can you recall a time when you departed from the belief that you can trust God with your circumstances? Write down the details of how your heart departed.

"When the people saw that Moses delayed in coming down from the mountain, they gathered around Aaron and said to him, 'Come, make us a god who will go before us because this Moses, the man who brought us up from the land of Egypt—we don't know what has happened to him!' "
Exodus 32:1

Their foolish choices cost them the future that God had intended for them.

Idols

An idol is anything that replaces God in our hearts. God delivered the Israelites from slavery in Egypt, miraculously supplied them with daily food and water in the desert, and completely defeated their enemies. He unleashed 10 devastating plagues on the Egyptians and parted the Red Sea to miraculously provide their way of escape. Their relationship with Almighty God gave the Israelites access to inexhaustible provision and power. But when Moses ascended Mount Sinai to meet with God for 40 days, the Israelites grew restless. They wanted a god who would serve them rather than rule them, so they ordered Aaron to make them an idol (Exodus 32:1).

These people had walked through a sea, eaten food from heaven, and witnessed fire and lightning on the mountain of God; yet they readily departed from their relationship with God to worship a golden, man-made calf. In fact, God's people would repeatedly betray Him to embrace things that were lifeless and impotent. In Old Testament times people trusted in easily identifiable idols. Their foolish choices cost them the future that God had intended for them. The apostle Paul declared, "The wages of sin is death" (Romans 6:23). Turning from God always brings spiritual death. That is the only alternative to the life God offers.

Later, after Joshua brought the Israelites into the promised land, they continually repeated the deadly cycle of apostasy. They temporarily walked with God, experiencing the victorious and abundant life He promised. But then, as the Book of Judges repeatedly states, "another generation rose up who did not know the Lord or the works He had done for Israel. The Israelites did what was evil in the Lord's sight. They worshiped the Baals" (Judges 2:10-11). Each time God disciplined His people for their rebellion, and they eventually cried out to Him for mercy. Then the Lord had compassion on them and rescued them once more. Tragically, it was never long before His people rejected Him again. This disastrous process was repeated for generations (see Judges 3:7-10,12-15; 4:1-4; 6:1-11; 8:33-35; 10:6-10; 13:1-5; 21:25). Church history echoes this same calamitous pattern of deliverance, idolatry, betrayal, and repentance. There is an unmistakable tendency for the human heart to gravitate away from God and toward something more tangible but far less satisfying.

Baal: Lord of Canaanite religion; Baal proved a great temptation for Israel

Place in order the following events in Israel's cycle of idolatry.
___ **God's people forsook their idols and returned to God.**
___ **God's people walked in intimate fellowship with God.**
___ **God's people once again enjoyed fellowship with God.**
___ **God's people's hearts turned away from God and trusted in idols.**

An idol is anything you trust in for which you should trust God. In the Old Testament an idol was a carved image fashioned into the likeness of a god. In modern times an idol can be money, friends, a job, popularity, possessions, a spouse, or innumerable other things. While these are not bad things in themselves, they can become idols in our lives if we place more trust and devotion in them than in God. We have certain needs that only God can meet. The world clamors to fill those needs with substitutes for God, but they do not satisfy. Nevertheless, we are continually tempted to place our trust in them.

Write your own definition of idol. An idol is:

Common Idols

Let's look at some of the substitutes for God listed in Scripture:

Underline each idol you find in the following verses.

"Know and recognize this: no sexually immoral or impure or greedy person, who is an idolater, has an inheritance in the kingdom of the Messiah and of God." Ephesians 5:5

"Cursed is the man who trusts in mankind, who makes human flesh his strength and turns his heart from the LORD." Jeremiah 17:5

"Some take pride in a chariot, and others in horses, but we take pride in the name of the LORD our God." Psalm 20:7

"No one can be a slave of two masters, since either he will hate one and love the other, or be devoted to one and despise the other. You cannot be slaves of God and of money." Matthew 6:24

"These people honor Me with their lips,
but their heart is far from Me.
They worship Me in vain,
teaching as doctrines the commands of men." Matthew 15:8–9

"The person who loves father or mother more than Me is not worthy of Me; the person who loves son or daughter more than Me is not worthy of Me." Matthew 10:37

"If anyone wants to come with Me, he must deny himself, take up his cross daily, and follow Me. For whoever wants to save his life will lose it, but whoever loses his life because of Me will save it." Luke 9:23–24

"You pore over the Scriptures because you think you have eternal life in them, yet they testify about Me. And you are not willing to come to Me that you may have life." John 5:39–40

"Do not love the world or the things that belong to the world. If anyone loves the world, love for the Father is not in him. Because everything that belongs to the world—the lust of the flesh, the lust of the eyes, and the pride in one's lifestyle—is not from the Father, but is from the world." 1 John 2:15–16

Let's look at a summary list of idols we can turn to:
   Sexual immorality (see Ephesians 5:5)
   Impurity (see Ephesians 5:5)
   People or their help (see Jeremiah 17:5)
   Political or military strength (see Psalm 20:7)
   Ritual worship and human teachings (see Matthew 15:8–9)
   Greed (see Matthew 6:24)
   Relationships such as family (see Matthew 10:37)
   Self (see Luke 9:23–24)
   Bible study for the attainment of mere knowledge (see John 5:39–40)

Do some of these surprise you? Not everything on the list is evil or wrong. However, if we allow anything to take God's place in our lives, our loyalty is misplaced.

This is not a complete list of substitutes for a love relationship with God. Below add any other idols that come to your mind. Remember, an idol is anything or any combination of things that captures your heart—your love—so that it is preeminent above God in your life.

Go back through the types of idols listed above. Put a check mark beside each one that has tempted you at some point in your life.

What voice seems to be the loudest in your life? List the top three influences on the decisions you make.

1.

2.

3.

We have a fatal tendency to turn away from trusting in God and placing our trust in people or things. Like the children of Israel, we think we know what is best for our lives. But none of them can meet the needs of our soul; only God can do that. Yet we foolishly abandon our relationship with God to find satisfaction in temporary, illusory, worldly substitutes. A sure sign that our heart has drifted away from God is when other voices or people have more influence in our lives than God does.

Encountering God in Prayer

Reflect on the various idols that have drawn you away from an intimate walk with God (p. 50). Consider God's provision that you abandoned to pursue your earthly idol. You cannot have God's provision and the benefit of an idol at the same time. You must choose one or the other. Take time to express to God in prayer your sorrow for ever turning your back on His loving provision for you. Acknowledge the reality that God and God alone knows what is best for you.

Day 4 # Religious Activity Versus Genuine Revival

Desperation for God

William M'Culloch was a preacher during the 18th century who was generally considered to have few gifts for ministry. But he loved his congregation in Cambuslang, Scotland, and wanted them to be fervent in their love for the Lord. Week after week this faithful preacher exhorted his people, but nothing changed in them. They came to church faithfully each week. They dutifully listened to his sermons. But it seemed as if it was merely habit and ritual. The people did not appear to encounter God at any level of their lives. One Sunday at the close of his sermon, M'Culloch saw that the service was ending, as usual, without a heartfelt response to God by the people. From a broken heart the weary pastor cried out, "Who has believed what we have heard? And who has the arm of the Lord been revealed to? Where is the fruit of my labor among this people?"[3]

Immediately, a conviction from the Holy Spirit swept across the congregation. Soon the auditorium was filled with the sounds of anguished weeping from those

> *A sure sign that our heart has drifted away from God is when other voices or people have more influence in our lives than God does.*

convicted of their sin. A great movement of God ensued as people sincerely returned to God. Services were held daily for seven months. Crowds swelled to as many as 20,000 in one meeting as people from all over the countryside traveled to worship with the people where the Spirit of God was clearly at work.[4]

When revival comes, it exposes religious activity that has been merely ritual and ceremony devoid of genuine fellowship with God. To some, Christianity means attending church, observing traditions, and keeping moral standards. But genuine Christianity is a personal relationship with Almighty God. We can be tempted to substitute religion for relationship. We are like the Pharisees, to whom Jesus said, "You pore over the Scriptures because you think you have eternal life in them, yet they testify about Me. And you are not willing to come to Me that you may have life" (John 5:39-40). Isn't it ironic that we can be exposed to the Scriptures—even study God's Word as the Pharisees did—and yet miss the Author who is in our midst?

We can be tempted to substitute religion for relationship.

List the most common forms for religious activity happening around you or in your own life.

Consider your own religious activities. If you discover some that are actually separating you from God, what changes will you make in them?

The Woman at the Well

On a trip through Samaria, Jesus stopped to rest at Jacob's well near the town of Sychar. As a woman came to draw water, Jesus asked her for a drink and then guided her into a discussion about living water.

In your Bible read John 4:10-23. What alternatives to a divine relationship had the woman accepted?

The Samaritan woman obviously had an enormous void in her life that she had unsuccessfully attempted to fill with a succession of husbands. When one man couldn't meet her deep longings, she looked for another. By the time she met Jesus, she was living with partner number six.

Today large numbers of people are turning to sexual relationships or other forms of human relationships to satisfy needs only God can meet. No human can fulfill the spiritual longing that is present in every person. God reserves the right to that deep, personal place in our hearts. Yet we seek to comfort ourselves in relationships, passions, pleasure, academics, sports, or various other things. None of these satisfy our spiritual thirst for living water. Only Jesus can meet that need in our lives.

How do parents sometimes seek purpose for their own lives through their children's activities?

What about spouses through one another?

The Samaritan woman also discussed religious worship practices with Jesus. Did you notice that the focus of her question was not on God? She was concerned about the place of worship and external rituals. For her, worship was about traditional religious activities. She knew nothing about a vibrant relationship with God. She had opinions about God, and yet she did not recognize the Son of God when He was standing next to her. But her demeanor completely changed once Jesus opened her eyes to the truth! At last—here is what she had been missing for years (see John 4:28-29).

Religious activity and tradition can never replace a relationship with God. No wonder multitudes of people reject the religion and stuffy rituals of those who claim to worship God but who have no relationship with Him! Religious activities abound today. Millions of people attend church every week but do not experience God working in their lives. Nothing can set people free from sin besides actually knowing and experiencing the living God. Why would we exchange a vital relationship with the living Lord for a set of religious activities? We can grow so busy being religious that we fail to experience life in Him.

Substitutes for God

A major tragedy of the Christian community is that individuals and churches often exchange work, ritual, religious activity, advertising, buildings, and programs for a love relationship with God. Whereas we once turned to Him, we now look to someone or something else.

We live in a day of rampant materialism. God's people often become as enamored with trinkets and entrapped by worldly comforts as unbelievers. Notice Scripture's warnings:

> *"Be careful that you don't forget the LORD your God by failing to keep His command—the ordinances and statutes—I am giving you today. When you eat and are full, and build beautiful houses to live in, and your herds and flocks grow large, and your silver and gold multiply, and everything else you have increases, be careful that your heart doesn't become proud and you forget the LORD your God. ... You may say to yourself, 'My power and my own ability have gained this wealth for me.'"* Deuteronomy 8:11–17

Look back over Deuteronomy 8:11-17 and underline everything that could cause people to forget the Lord.

"Then the woman left her water jar, went into town, and told the men, 'Come, see a man who told me everything I ever did! Could this be the Messiah?' "
John 4:28-29

List three things that cause people today to turn their trust and devotion away from God.

1.

2.

3.

Go back and place an _R_ beside relationships, _RA_ beside religious activities, _M_ beside material possessions, and _A_ beside attitudes. Add tags of your own if needed.

Do any of the items on your list above presently apply to your life? Pride causes us to exaggerate our own abilities. Wealth often leads to a desire for more possessions. Jesus said, "Watch out and be on guard against all greed because one's life is not in the abundance of his possessions" (Luke 12:15).

God loves us and wants us to choose life, not destruction. He gives two options; there is no compromise. God desires a love relationship with His people. We are to love Him wholeheartedly and obey Him fully. Then Scripture promises we will experience abundant life. Only God can offer us life because the Lord Himself is life.

Any departure from Christ is serious. In fact, it can be fatal. Today around the world many Christians are experiencing grievous consequences for their sin, while numerous churches are dying and disbanding. At the heart of this malady is the refusal by believers to repent and return to their first love for Christ. Because they are not walking closely with God, they are in no position to serve Him. God is extremely patient, but He will eventually discipline people when they continue to disobey and reject Him (see 2 Peter 3:9).

> _"The Lord does not delay His promise, as some understand delay, but is patient with you, not wanting any to perish, but all to come to repentance."_
> **2 Peter 3:9**

Ways We Wander

What does it look like in the modern church when God's people try to offer substitutes for His presence, purposes, ways, provision, and guidance?

Read the following lists of verses to see examples of ways we move away from God and His work in us. As you read the verses, make notes in the margin about how you should guard your relationship with God.

Substitutes for God's Presence
— **Trusting in theatrical elements so that people have a profound experience during the worship service** (see 1 Kings 18:26-29)
— **Depending on emotional worship songs and using manipulation to evoke responses from people in worship services rather than relying on the Holy Spirit to convict of sin** (see 1 Corinthians 4:20)
— **Trying to pressure people to do what we think is right or making them feel guilty for their sin rather than relying on the Holy Spirit to work in their hearts** (see John 16:8)

Substitutes for God's Purposes

—Conducting baptism and the Lord's Supper services as tradition or ritual when God intended them to be times of public testimony, remembrance of Him, personal examination, and renewal of fellowship (see 1 Corinthians 11:24-26)

—Spending much of our time and resources on ourselves while ignoring justice for the oppressed or meeting the needs of the poor (see Galatians 2:10)

—Carrying out evangelistic visits primarily to boost church attendance rather than to lead people to God (see 2 Corinthians 5:14-15)

Substitutes for God's Ways

—Walking by sight when God's Word instructs us to live by faith (see Hebrews 11:1,6)

—Affirming and focusing on self when God says to deny self (see Matthew 16:24)

—Pursuing positions of influence and prestige when God instructs us to humble ourselves (see James 4:10)

—Clinging to what we have, though Christ said to give it away for the Kingdom's sake (see Matthew 16:25)

—Coercing people to serve on committees rather than praying for God to send forth laborers (see Matthew 9:37-38)

Substitutes for God's Provision

—Trusting in our limited resources without asking God to provide (see Psalm 20:7)

—Never attempting to do anything for God unless we already have all the resources needed in advance (see Hebrews 11:6)

—Quitting when problems arise rather than trusting that God will provide a way (see Philippians 4:19)

Substitutes for God's Guidance

—Turning to counselors and consultants but not spending significant time in prayer (see Jeremiah 33:3)

—Conducting a survey of our community or taking a survey of our congregation to determine what our church should do but offering only superficial, token prayers to God (see Jeremiah 33:3)

—Listening to parents, spouse, friends, financial advisers, or others but not earnestly seeking God's will in a major decision we are facing (see Matthew 7:7)

Look back over the substitutes listed. Put a check mark next to any that you personally and/or your church is guilty of.

God's Word warns of the danger we face when we take our eyes off Him and His priorities: "If you ever forget the LORD your God and go after other gods to worship and bow down to them, I testify against you today that you will perish" (Deuteronomy 8:19). You may consider this admonishment to be extremely severe. It is. It reveals how seriously God views sin and rebellion. The Bible teaches that God is jealous of our love (see Exodus 20:5; Deuteronomy 4:24). He created us and deserves our devotion. Therefore, He is relentlessly opposed to anything that challenges His rightful place in our lives.

This world is an arena for self. Every new generation strives harder to make life easier, safer, longer, and more comfortable. The Bible doesn't tell us to live in the Dark Ages or to stop learning, growing, and progressing. However, God's Word is filled with warnings against misplacing the trust of our heart. Every generation faces the same choice: self or God. Many Christians and churches today have no idea how self-centered they actually are.

Every generation faces the same choice: self or God.

Encountering God in Prayer

Ask the Lord to show you anything that has become a substitute for Him in your life. What is the first place you turn when you face a problem or undergo a crisis? That indicates where you put your greatest trust. Do you instinctively turn to God whenever you are in need? If not, take time in prayer to repent to God for relying on anyone in His place. Let God draw your heart back to Him in dependence.

Day 5 # God's Cure for Backsliding

Struggling with Anger

backsliding: term used to describe faithlessness to God by serving other gods and living immoral lives.

Frank grew up in the tumultuous home of an abusive father. Though he despised the anger that victimized him as a child, when he became a husband and father, he also habitually exploded with rage, terrifying his wife and children. Afterward he felt horrible and promised his wife never to do it again. But he did. Frank was a Christian. He prayed during worship services and asked God to forgive him for his angry outbursts. He promised his wife that things would be different in the future. He talked with his pastor and admitted he had a problem. But despite his best efforts to stop abusing his family, something inevitably pushed him over the edge, and he erupted even more angrily than before. It became a routine experience to see Frank at the front of the church tearfully praying. Those who knew him understood he must be confessing another lapse in self-control.

Only God has a cure for backsliding.

The violent cycle continued for years until Frank experienced a crisis so devastating that he finally released complete control of his life to God. To this point of his life, Frank had been in control, trying by his best efforts to reform his sinful behavior. But the result was always the same. He inevitably and painfully backslid into the same destructive behavior. Frank came to understand that only God has a cure for backsliding.

Does the above story parallel your experience? Is there a sin in your life that you struggle to conquer? Is your Christian walk characterized by dramatic ups and downs consisting of periods of closeness to God and times when He seems distant?

On the chart below, graph your Christian growth in maturity over the past 10 years. Plot your Christian growth, year by year, based on whether you grew closer or fell away from God.

■————————————————————●

Closer to God   **Further**

What strikes you about your spiritual pilgrimage over the past decade? Does your spiritual journey reflect—

[ ] **a stagnant walk with God?**
[ ] **a plateaued walk with God?**
[ ] **ups and downs?**
[ ] **minimal growth?**
[ ] **exciting, dramatic growth?**
[ ] **consistent, regular growth?**

What kind of spiritual growth do you think God intends for you in the near future?

Backsliding

The process of backsliding is a gradual one. It is much like the way a marriage can break down over time from devotion, to inattention, to apathy, to neglect, to antagonism, and finally to rejection. Forsaking a loved one does not normally occur with a solitary act but through a process that, if left unchecked, leads to enormous pain. The fundamental issue in backsliding is not primarily a struggle with sin but a departure from a close, devoted walk with God.

Read what God said to the nations of Israel and Judah when they turned their devotion away from Him:

> *"Have you seen what backsliding Israel has done? She has gone up on every high mountain and under every green tree, and there played the harlot. And I said, after she had done all these things, 'Return to Me.' But she did not return. ... Her treacherous sister Judah did not fear, but went and played the harlot also. ... Her treacherous sister Judah has not turned to Me with her whole heart, but in pretense. ...'*
> *'Return, backsliding Israel,' says the Lord;*
> *'I will not cause My anger to fall on you.*
> *For I am merciful,' says the Lord;*
> *'I will not remain angry forever.*
> *Only acknowledge your iniquity,*

That you have transgressed against the L<small>ORD</small> your God,
And have scattered your charms
To alien deities under every green tree,
And you have not obeyed My voice,' says the L<small>ORD</small>. ...
'Return you backsliding children,
and I will heal your backslidings.'" Jeremiah 3:6-22, NKJV

In response to their unfaithfulness, what did God want the people to do?

Write your own definition of what it means to backslide.

God calls it a heartbreaking betrayal.

Did you notice the passion with which God appealed to His wayward people, encouraging them to return to Him? Clearly, God's desire is not to be separated from His people. Spiritual backsliding is serious because it is not simply a moral lapse or a rough spot in the Christian life. God calls it a heartbreaking betrayal.

How tragic that Almighty God must urge His people to return to their love relationship with Him. One would think we would be eager to enjoy such a relationship with God. Yet inevitably, our hearts drift away. Despite our declarations of loyalty to Him, we often turn away from Him and gravitate toward substitutes for God in our lives.

Symptoms of Backsliding

What are the signs that an individual or a congregation has drifted from God? Two clear indicators are evident: (1) disobedience and (2) substitutes for God. As a doctor looks for symptoms to diagnosis someone's illness, let's probe some of the manifestations of a heart that has departed from the Lord.

First, notice the clear connection Jesus made between obedience and love:

"If you love Me, you will keep My commandments." John 14:15

"The one who has My commands and keeps them is the one who loves Me." John 14:21

According to the previous verses, what is the proof that someone truly loves God?

The symptom is disobedience; the malady is a lack of love.

Jesus announced it was spiritually impossible to simultaneously love Him and disobey Him. The symptom is disobedience; the malady is a lack of love. Love will obey. We may strongly protest and say, "Lord, it's not that I don't love you; it's just that I'm having trouble obeying you." God would say, "If you are struggling to follow Me, it is because you do not love Me."

If you misunderstand this truth, you will always be frustrated in your attempts to connect with God. You will vainly attempt to reform your behavior, and you will inevitably fail. In our Christian lives we tend to treat symptoms rather than causes. A God-initiated revival will treat the cause of our spiritual malady.

> **Managing our behavior is much easier than changing our hearts. Put an *X* beside examples of behavior management and circle those that represent heart changes.**
> > **Quit a bad habit**
> > **Worship with passion**
> > **Tithe in order to enjoy God's blessings**
> > **Join a Bible-study class to increase knowledge**
> > **Serve in a church ministry that no one else will do**
> > **Pray with increased faith**

Did you find it difficult in some cases to discern between heart change and behavior modification? The lines can be fuzzy because we hope all changes occur at a heart level. As individual believers, we must search out the *why* of our changes. Do we change because our love for God is increasing or because our lives are simply becoming uncomfortable?

Do you know how to solve a disobedience problem? Return to your love relationship with God. That will resolve the obedience problems in your life. God declared He would arrest the people's spiral into disobedience (Jeremiah 3:22). However, first they had to return to Him wholeheartedly (Jeremiah 3:7,12,22). We cannot transform our own hearts. Our hearts are thoroughly wicked and deceptive (Jeremiah 17:9). We may think we have returned to God when in fact we have only gone through the perfunctory motions of trying to adjust our behavior (Jeremiah 3:10). Even the strongest resolve to do better will be ineffective. Unless the Holy Spirit radically transforms our hearts, we will continue to backslide over and over again in our walk with God. No superficial cure will do. Only a divine transformation of our heart will cure us of our chronic spiritual departures.

> **Various attitudes and activities can be the result of our wandering hearts. What must change in a person's life to stop the cycle of continual backsliding?**

All of these things can affect our relationship with God. However, if we love God with all of our heart, mind, soul, and strength (see Mark 12:30), our love for Him can overcome any of these issues. Whenever our love for God begins to weaken, these issues will begin to negatively affect our walk with God.

"'Return, you backsliding children, and I will heal your backslidings.' 'Indeed we do come to You, For You are the LORD our God.'"
Jeremiah 3:22, NKJV

"'Her treacherous sister Judah has not turned to Me with her whole heart, but in pretense,' says the LORD."
Jeremiah 3:10, NKJV

"Love the Lord your God with all your heart, with all your soul, with all your mind, and with all your strength."
Mark 12:30

Recognize Backsliding

How can you tell whether you or your church has drifted away from a close walk with God? One way to recognize spiritual regression is to consider if there is something God asked of you in the past that you obeyed without question but now resist. For example, perhaps in the past you readily forgave others because your own sense of being graciously pardoned by God was so strong. But now you find that you are harboring resentment toward several persons who have offended you. Perhaps you once enthusiastically spoke about your faith with others, but now you hesitate to talk about what Christ means to you? When Christ gives a command in His Word and you begin to argue with Him, it demonstrates that your heart has shifted.

Examine the following Scriptures to determine how you or your church is demonstrating your love for Christ.

- Do you love your fellow believers unconditionally? "I give you a new commandment: love one another. Just as I have loved you, you must also love one another" (John 13:34).
- Do you forgive others? "Whenever you stand praying, if you have anything against anyone, forgive him, so that your Father in heaven will also forgive you your wrongdoing" (Mark 11:25).
- Is your church known as a congregation that prays? "It is written, 'My house will be a house of prayer'" (Luke 19:46).
- Do you give generously to the Lord's work while also practicing justice, mercy, and faith? "Woe to you, ... hypocrites! You pay a tenth of mint, dill, and cumin, yet you have neglected the more important matters of the law—justice, mercy, and faith. These things should have been done without neglecting the others" (Matthew 23:23).
- Are you actively seeking to make disciples of the nations, including those represented in your community? "Go, therefore, and make disciples of all nations, baptizing them ... [and] teaching them to observe everything I have commanded you" (Matthew 28:19-20).
- Are you serving Christ in the power of His Spirit? "You will receive power when the Holy Spirit has come upon you, and you will be my witnesses in Jerusalem, in all Judea and Samaria, and to the end of the earth" (Acts 1:8).
- Are you experiencing genuine unity with other believers in your church, with other churches, and with Christians in other denominations?

Which of the previous verses address symptoms of backsliding in your life?

If you noticed that you or your church is no longer obeying the Lord's commands as diligently as you used to, it is a clear sign that you have departed from God. Churches can depart from God just as individuals can. For example, many people in a congregation may sincerely seek God's will and sense He is leading their church in a particular direction. However, some members may worry about the cost or may launch a storm of protest at the direction being proposed. If the congregation decides to appease the naysayers and not move forward with what God told them to do, it indicates that the heart of the church has begun to shift. Over time a church can so deviate from God's will that even those who were once receptive to Him become disoriented to Him. In a misguided quest to pursue church unity at all costs, many congregations have inadvertently chosen corporate disobedience. God's Word warns, "Watch out, brothers, so that there won't be in any of you an evil, unbelieving heart that departs from the living God. But encourage each other daily, while it is called today, so that none of you is hardened by sin's deception" (Hebrews 3:12-13).

> **What might be some other signs that a church has departed from a close walk with the Lord?**

> **What are signs that a church is remaining focused on God? For example, think about the number of conversions, church plants, or mission trips in recent years.**

The testimony of Scripture clearly reveals that the Lord is grieved when His people edge away from their close relationship with Him. Backsliding is not something we can afford to treat carelessly. There can be devastating consequences. God takes our devotion to Him extremely seriously. So should we.

Encountering God in Prayer

Examine your heart and your relationship with God. Do you love Him as you should? Are you obeying Him? Are you walking closely with Him? Look at your responses to the activity on page 50 and identify ways you have substituted idols for God's presence, purposes, ways, provisions, or guidance. Examine any evidence of backsliding you identified on page 60. Bring these issues before God and repent. Confess your love for Him and commit to obey Him because of that love. Ask Him to help you identify changes you need to make in your life and to give you spiritual strength and wisdom to make these changes.

Backsliding is not something we can afford to treat carelessly.

1. Jonathan Edwards, *Works of President Edwards* (New York: Leavitt and Allen, 1857), 3:239.
2. Ibid., 3:235.
3. Richard Owen Roberts, ed., *Scotland Saw His Glory* (Wheaton, IL: International Awakening Press, 1995), 132.
4. Ibid., 137.

Session 2
Small-Group Discussion Guide

❧ † ❧

Open in prayer.

Ahead of time, ask someone to be prepared to pray. Invite prayer requests and ask the group for prayer requests that pertain to personal and corporate revival. Listen for how God is presently working in their lives through the study so that the group will know how to pray for them. Once people have had an opportunity to share, call on the person appointed to pray.

View Session 2 of the Teaching DVD

Truths to Remember

Scriptures to Read

Quotes to Remember

Actions to Take

If you missed this session, go to *www.lifeway.com/freshencounter* to download this and any other session of *Fresh Encounter.*

Discussion Guide

Ask group members what they learned about the heart this week. Take 5 to 10 minutes for individuals to share what God taught them through the study.

Could you identify with the material from your own experience? Can you give any examples?

Ask members to share their reactions to the DVD segment.

What encouraged you?

What challenged you?

Read Jeremiah 17:9. What are some common ways that our heart's desires for earthly things move us away from a close relationship to Christ?

In the video, Richard told the story of the time he knew for certain of his love for his wife. What is the evidence in the life of a Christian that expresses their love for God?

We are warned that broken cisterns are the all-too common substitute for a refreshing relationship with God.

What broken cisterns (or idols) do people turn to in order to find spiritual answers?

Why are people so prone to turn to earthly substitutes rather than receive what God offers to give them—Himself?

What must we do to return to the "living water" of Christ?

Invite members to show the group the chart of their Christian growth (p. 57). Have them briefly explain their journey of growth, stagnation, or backsliding.

It does not seem that people start out their walk with Christ with the intention of abandoning their relationship with Him. But our tendency is to wander away.

How does backsliding begin?

Why do people tend to backslide in their Christian faith?

What can a church family do to aid believers when they become disobedient to Christ?

Look at the list of scriptures on page 60. Discuss how your church compares to this list in its worship of God, ministry to one another, and efforts to make disciples of people in the community.

Invite any final comments or observations.

Close in prayer.

UNIT 3: GOD'S LOVING DISCIPLINE

Scripture-Memory Verses

"My son, do not take the Lord's discipline lightly, or faint when you are reproved by Him; for the Lord disciplines the one He loves, and punishes every son whom He receives."

HEBREWS 12:5-6

Unit Overview

DAY 1: THE NATURE OF GOD

DAY 2: GOD'S DISCIPLINE AND JUDGMENT

DAY 3: THE MEANS OF GOD'S DISCIPLINE AND JUDGMENT

DAY 4: SPIRITUAL WARFARE AND GOD'S DISCIPLINE

DAY 5: RESPONDING TO GOD'S DISCIPLINE

Cleansing by Washing with Water Through the Word

THIS WEEK WE WILL DEAL WITH WHAT MANY CONSIDER AN UNWELCOME LESSON—GOD'S DISCIPLINE. Why do we so desperately avoid something that can do so much good in our lives? Again, Ephesians 5 states that Christ's intention is to present us in purity so that we will be radiant in His sight: *"Christ loved the church and gave Himself for her, to make her holy, cleansing her in the washing of water by the word. He did this to present the church to Himself in splendor, without spot or wrinkle or any such thing, but holy and blameless"* (Ephesians 5:25-27).

Wash Out

We need to have rebelliousness washed out of our lives. This week consider what sins might be bringing God's discipline to your life, your family, and your church. Prepare yourself for an unflinching gaze into why God's discipline must come and how you can be restored to an intimate relationship with Christ.

Soak In

What are the good things God desires to teach you through His discipline? Pray that you will quickly learn those lessons as you meditate on His Word.

→ **Hebrews 12:5-11**

→ **Isaiah 59:2**

→ **Revelation 2:5**

→ **Luke 19:43-44**

→ **1 Peter 4:7**

→ **James 5:9**

Keep the verses above in mind as you work through the Bible studies this week. Use the space below to keep a list of the specific lessons you learn from your studies and how God is applying these lessons to your life.

God's Discipline

The Civil War, culminating years of turmoil, was the most devastating crisis the United States had ever faced. The issue of slavery was intensely divisive. Because the Industrial Age created unprecedented wealth, pursuing money and pleasure became a consuming passion. Churches were in decline. Public morality had descended to shocking levels. The outbreak of the Civil War ushered in unimaginable devastation. Families were ripped apart. Hundreds of thousands of America's young men were slaughtered. The government sought answers to how and why something so cataclysmic could happen within their nation. Ultimately, both houses of Congress issued a proclamation, signed by President Abraham Lincoln, for a national day of prayer on August 12, 1861. Carefully read that publication and consider its applicability to our present day.

PROCLAMATION OF A NATIONAL FAST DAY, AUGUST 12, 1861

"Whereas a joint committee of both Houses of Congress has waited on the President of the United States, and requested him to 'recommend a day of public humiliation, prayer and fasting, to be observed by the people of the United States with religious solemnities, and the offering of fervent supplications to Almighty God' ...

"It is fit and becoming in all people, at all times, to acknowledge and revere the Supreme Government of God; to bow in humble submission to his chastisements; to confess and deplore their sins and transgressions in the full conviction that the fear of the Lord is the beginning of wisdom; and to pray, with all fervency and contrition, for the pardon of their past offences. ...

"When our own beloved Country, once, by the blessing of God, united, prosperous and happy, is now afflicted with faction and civil war, it is peculiarly fit for us to recognize the hand of God in this terrible visitation, and in sorrowful remembrance of our own faults and crimes as a nation and as individuals, to humble ourselves before Him, and to pray for His mercy. ...

"Therefore, I, Abraham Lincoln, President of the United States, do appoint the last Thursday in September next as a day of humiliation, prayer and fasting for all the people of the nation."[1]

❧ † ❧

Day 1 The Nature of God

A Heavenly Father

AT A CONFERENCE, HENRY WAS APPROACHED BY A YOUNG WOMAN IN TEARS. She explained that her father had abandoned her family when she was young. She had never known him and though she had earnestly longed for contact from him it never came. As a result she felt unloved and unlovable. After studying the course _Experiencing God_, she discovered that God was a loving Father. Looking back, she realized that God had been pursuing her all of her life. He had taken an active interest in her and had often expressed His love to her in numerous ways. While she had not had an earthly father to correct her or to teach her how to live, she had received the active involvement of her Heavenly Father. When she had drifted into harmful activities and unhealthy relationships, God had orchestrated events to bring her back to Himself. When she had experienced need, God had surrounded her with people to help. Rather than viewing God's discipline and correction of her as negative, she realized that God's active involvement in her life was a continual expression of His love and interest in her. She told Henry, "Thank you for helping me realize I have a Father who loves me and will do whatever is necessary for me to experience abundant life."

> **Think about the positive nature of God's discipline. Scripture teaches that He does what is necessary to steer us toward His best for us. How has God worked in your life to ensure you remained in His will?**

> **Go back to the illustration at the beginning of the unit and underline the statements the American congress made concerning God's judgment on their nation. How does your nation compare to the United States immediately preceding the Civil War? Is it in better or worse condition?**

Many Christians have lost the fear of God. People no longer believe God disciplines His people. Many think the God of judgment and wrath is confined to the ancient pages of the Old Testament. They believe the God of the New Testament is characterized only by love and grace. Such thinking reveals a skewed and limited knowledge of what Scripture reveals about God. But Scripture teaches that God said, "I, Yahweh, have not changed" (Malachi 3:6).

God is beyond our understanding. Yet, He has revealed His character to us in Scripture. The fundamental essence of His nature is love (1 John 4:8). He does nothing apart from pure, unfailing, perfect love. He forever proved His lovingkindness through Jesus' death on a cross (Romans 8:31-32). He is compassionate, patient, and slow to anger. Likewise, God is absolutely holy, pure, and just (1 Peter 5:15-16). God perfectly balances infinite love with absolute righteousness. His judgments are as equally righteous as they are gracious. He seldom gives us the punishment we deserve. He freely forgives us when we repent and return to Him.

Notice what Scripture indicates about God's nature as He interacts with people:

"I knew that You are a merciful and compassionate God, slow to become angry, rich in faithful love, and One who relents from sending disaster." Jonah 4:2

"Dear friends, let us love one another, because love is from God, and everyone who loves has been born of God and knows God." 1 John 4:7

"I am the LORD, showing faithful love, justice, and righteousness on the earth, for I delight in these things. This is the LORD's declaration." Jeremiah 9:24

"Against You—You alone—I have sinned
and done this evil in Your sight.
So You are right when You pass sentence;
You are blameless when You judge." Psalm 51:4

"The word of the LORD is right,
and all His work is trustworthy.
He loves righteousness and justice;
the earth is full of the LORD's unfailing love." Psalm 33:4–5

"The LORD sits enthroned forever;
He has established His throne for judgment.
He judges the world with righteousness;
He executes judgment on the peoples with fairness." Psalm 9:7–8

"The LORD of Hosts is exalted by His justice,
and the holy God is distinguished by righteousness." Isaiah 5:16

Look back through the preceding verses and underline the numerous revelations about God's nature.

God's Nature Revealed

The Bible, from Genesis to Revelation, clearly teaches that God disciplines His people; yet many Christians struggle with this truth. Much of our confusion about God's discipline comes from our misunderstanding of God's nature. Two major aspects of God's nature shed light on the way He disciplines His people.

God Is Holy

God is absolutely pure and holy (see 1 Peter 1:15-16). Therefore, He is entirely different from us and set apart from His creation. God is eternally consistent. Unlike people, He does not change the rules or adjust His standards over time. Because God is holy, He never condones sin or evil (see Psalm 97:10; 119:104). Sin brings death (see Romans 6:23). Sin caused the suffering and death of God's only Son (see Romans 6:10). Sin has been responsible for the anguish of countless people from every age. God's holiness means that He is rightly and vehemently opposed to every form of sin.

Some seek to portray God solely as a God of grace, based on the attributes of love and mercy portrayed by His Son, Jesus, in the New Testament. However, when Jesus came to earth, He was not only full of grace but also full of truth (see John 1:14). Jesus' holiness compelled Him to be wholly committed to truth and always opposed to falsehood. Because God continues to be holy, He is the enemy of sin in your life, your church, and your nation.

When you think of God, what is the first characteristic that comes to mind?

Love   Forgiveness   Grace   Other:

Why do you immediately think of that trait?

How has God's holiness affected the way you relate to Him?

Is God's holiness an attractive or offensive quality in your eyes? Why?

God Is Love

God is also a loving Father. The fundamental essence of His nature is love (see 1 John 4:7-8). He does nothing apart from pure, unfailing, perfect love. He is compassionate, patient, and slow to anger. Even the reluctant prophet Jonah knew that God desires restoration over the destruction of sinners (see Jonah 4:2).

In the Old Testament, we read of God's love time after time as He gently dealt with the Israelites. In fact, many of their songs recorded in Psalms dealt with God's patient love toward their need for correction. In Psalm 103:11-14, God's forgiving nature is painted in this way:

*"As high as the heavens are above the earth,
so great is His faithful love toward those who fear Him.
As far as the east is from the west,
so far has He removed
our transgressions from us.*

*As a father has compassion on his children,
so the Lord has compassion on those who fear Him.
For He knows what we are made of, remembering that we are dust."*

Even when we wander from a faithful relationship with God, He shows a fatherly compassion that draws us back. His love is so great that it separates us from our sin rather than allowing our sin to separate us from Himself.

God's lovingkindness culminated in Jesus' death on a cross (see Romans 8:31-32). He loves humans so much that He sent His Son to be sacrificed for our sin, allowing us a way to enjoy eternal life with Him (see John 3:16).

God's Loving Discipline

Many Christians have lost a fear of God and no longer believe God disciplines His people. Many think the God of judgment and wrath is confined to the ancient pages of the Old Testament. They believe the God of the New Testament is characterized only by love and grace that turn a blind eye to our faults. Such thinking reveals a skewed, limited knowledge of the Scripture. The writer of Hebrews reminds us, "Jesus Christ is the same yesterday, today, and forever" (13:8). The God we find in the New Testament is exactly the same God revealed in the pages of the Old Testament. He doesn't change.

Our unchanging God is holy, He must judge sin. Yet His judgment of believers' sin is tempered by love. God perfectly balances infinite love with absolute righteousness. Read Hebrews 12:5-11 in the margin to see how Scripture compares the Lord's admonishments to the way loving parents guide their children.

> **Hebrews 12:5-11 paints a portrait of a father who deeply cares about the activities of his children. In the past, you may not have considered that God is this concerned about your everyday activities. How does this passage increase your understanding of God's involvement in your life?**

Though difficult to endure, undergoing God's discipline is a sure sign that we are in a relationship with Him. When we are corrected by God, it is a sure sign that He is watching our lives and desires to direct our steps. Though the correction is not "enjoyable at the time" (Hebrews 12:11), it is a sure signal that God is active in our lives.

Unlike our earthly parents' motivations, God's love is extended through His discipline for eternal purposes. Sin carries us away from our identity in Christ. It robs us of the joy of being set apart for His kingdom's mission and purposes. But, the gift of God's discipline in our lives grants us something we could never earn on our own—sharing in the holiness of God! By submitting to God's corrective work in our lives, we are lifted from the mundane existence offered by sin and are enabled to live out God's plan through Christ's character empowered by the Spirit's indwelling presence. God's discipline is done out of love for our good.

*"You have forgotten the exhortation that addresses you as sons: My son, do not take the Lord's discipline lightly, or faint when you are reproved by Him; for the Lord disciplines the one He loves, and punishes every son whom He receives. Endure it as discipline: God is dealing with you as sons. For what son is there whom a father does not discipline? But if you are without discipline—which all receive—then you are illegitimate children and not sons. Furthermore, we had natural fathers discipline us, and we respected them. Shouldn't we submit even more to the Father of spirits and live? For they disciplined us for a short time based on what seemed good to them, but He does it for our benefit, so that we can share His holiness. No discipline seems enjoyable at the time, but painful. Later on, however, it yields the fruit of peace and righteousness to those who have been trained by it."
Hebrews 12:5-11*

As parents, we do not enjoy the process of disciplining our children. But we enjoy the results that come from proper discipline because we want the best for our children. The nature of God's love can be understood as His desire for our good.

Answer the following as true or false about God's discipline.

It comes from spite and hatred.	T	F
It is a sign of His disfavor.	T	F
It provides evidence of His love.	T	F
It allows us to experience abundant life.	T	F
It gives evidence of a relationship with God.	T	F

God's discipline is done out of love for our good.

God is perfect. He is simultaneously holy and loving. Even when He disciplines us, our Heavenly Father acts in perfect love. Just as loving parents oppose anything that robs their children of what is good, God adamantly renounces anything that keeps you from experiencing His will for your life. God would not be loving if He remained indifferent to your harmful choices. His love is displayed through the many interventions He enacts to protect us from sin's effects and the justice we rightly deserve.

The Fruit of Discipline

God's discipline is designed to lead us to repentance. His judgments are as gracious as they are righteous. He seldom gives us the punishment we deserve. He freely forgives us when we repent and return to Him. God's hope for any discipline upon our lives is to bring about the fruit of repentance. He has a gracious desire for His people to return to Him and enjoy the fellowship that was once lost.

Take a moment and think about the news you heard today. What should our nation's reaction be if Lincoln's proclamation were made today?

What feelings arise in you when you ponder God's discipline?

Has God disciplined you? If so, what is one way He did?

As a perfect Father, God loves us too much to allow us to embrace sin and to live in rebellion against Him. As a loving Father, He disciplines us to the extent necessary to break down our defiance and draw us back. Every time you experience God's discipline, rejoice that He has given you evidence once more that you are His child!

Encountering God in Prayer

How is God presently working in your life? Is He disciplining you? If He is, how are you responding? Are you resisting or yielding to His correction? Have you grown bitter, or have you embraced God as your Father who loves you and is willing to do whatever is necessary to bring you back to Himself? Take some time to thank God for specific ways He has been a loving Father to you.

Day 2 # God's Discipline and Judgment

Every time you experience God's discipline, rejoice ...

Spiritual Warfare?

Henry once had a pastor relate to him the many painful experiences he had undergone. Each of his children had abandoned their faith and was living an immoral lifestyle. His marriage had crumbled, and many church members were calling for his resignation. As he faced mounting pressures, his health had deteriorated. Grimly, the man looked at Henry and proclaimed, "I have been in the midst of intense spiritual warfare." But had he? Perhaps he was too quick to assume that his three wayward children, his failed marriage, and his dwindling congregation were solely the result of Satan's activity. This man gave plentiful evidence through his attitudes and continual spiritual defeats that he was under God's judgment and was reaping what he had sown. It is imperative that we clearly recognize when God is disciplining us.

Discipline, Judgment, and Final Judgment

Discipline and judgment are two different ways God relates to people in their sin. Each has a definitive use in God's work among humanity.

God's Discipline

Discipline is for God's children. There is no need to convince those outside of His family to act as if they belong to it. Notice what God said through the prophet Amos:

> *"I have known only you*
> *out of all the clans of the earth;*
> *therefore, I will punish you for all your iniquities."* Amos 3:2

It is imperative that we clearly recognize when God is disciplining us.

Once people become Christians, they are transformed into new creatures and are God's adopted children (see Romans 8:16-17; 2 Corinthians 5:17). They cannot lose their salvation, but they can drift away from God and become embroiled in sin. When this happens, God brings circumstances into their lives that make their sinful choices intolerable and awaken their sense of dependency on Him. Discipline is God's means of turning His rebellious children away from sin and back to fellowship with Him. It discourages us from sinning and encourages us to obey Him once more. God's discipline is not intended to paralyze us with shame, but it produces godly conviction and promotes repentance from sin.

What are some reasons God disciplines us?

Why would God's children not willingly want to follow His will?

Because God loves His children, He will do whatever is necessary to turn them from destructive ways. Nevertheless, it is possible for Christians to resist God's chastening as He seeks to turn them back to Himself. People can harden their hearts to God's truth and refuse to humble themselves, regardless of how uncomfortable God's discipline makes them. Although God is patient, He will not allow His children to continually profane His name and sully His reputation by misrepresenting Him.

Describe a time when God disciplined you. If you cannot recall a time, consider Hebrews 12:5-12 again from page 71 as to how you might become more sensitive to God's work in your life.

God's Judgment

God uses judgment, on the other hand, for the purpose of punishment rather than reform. He applies judgment when His patience with rebellion has come to an end and He vindicates His holy name. Take a few moments to read Ezekiel 36:16-23 in your Bible.

God also uses judgment to warn people of the grave consequences of unrepented sin. This form of judgment can also be described as remedial or temporal judgment (see Amos 3:2). Focused on our present life, it brings severe consequences to those who blatantly mock and disregard God's standards. This judgment causes others to take notice of what happens when people flaunt their sin before a holy God.

God may inflict judgment on unbelievers as a warning of sin's ultimate consequences. For example, in Genesis 19 the wickedness of Sodom and Gomorrah was so detestable that God brought judgment on both cities and destroyed them. The people of these cities had become so depraved that God severely judged them. Judgment can be withheld if people repent, as with the city of Nineveh in Jonah's day. However, if people do not turn from their sin, God's response is severe.

God also judges believers when they turn away from Him and refuse to repent, providing an example to deter others from committing the same offense. Such was the case with Achan (see Joshua 7) as well as Ananias and Sapphira.

God uses judgment, on the other hand, for the purpose of punishment rather than reform.

Ananias and his wife, Sapphira, were members of the church in Jerusalem. They sold some land but brought only a portion of the proceeds to contribute to the church. However, they led their fellow church members to believe they were giving everything to the Lord. They may have been expecting praise and public recognition. Read their story from Acts 5 in the margin.

The Jerusalem church was young and learning how to walk with the Holy Spirit. A wicked influence of deceit could corrupt the entire congregation and its mission to take the gospel throughout the world. God's people had to learn they could not treat the Holy Spirit lightly (see Matthew 12:31). Because their sin could have an exponential influence, God immediately executed judgment on the sinful couple. The result was that "great fear came on the whole church and on all who heard these things" (Acts 5:11). Moreover, Scripture indicates: "Believers were added to the Lord in increasing numbers—crowds of both men and women" (Acts 5:14). When God's people gained a healthy reverence for the Holy Spirit, they experienced His power mightily working through them, drawing others to Christ as a result.

God's judgment of Christians is temporal in that it is confined to their lives on earth and does not follow them into eternity. When God judges Christians, they do not lose their salvation; but they can forfeit their possessions, reputation, health, and even their lives. In 1 Corinthians 3:15, Paul taught the early church to invest in work that will not be burned up in God's refining fire on the day of judgment. Our relationships, work, and ministry should be carefully tested to ensure that it measures up with God's work in His kingdom. Ultimately, we will answer for all of our actions in this life and rewarded for what we have done according to God's will (see 2 Corinthians 5:10). As we have learned, discipline is not pleasant, but an unexamined life is an eternal tragedy.

Name some of the reasons God will bring judgment on people in this life rather than waiting until the final judgment to give people what they deserve.

God's Final Judgment

Final judgment is reserved for unbelievers at the close of history. The term final indicates there are no appeals and no further opportunities to repent or correct one's ways. Those who refuse to accept Christ's offer of salvation will be sentenced to irrevocable, eternal punishment (see Matthew 25:31-46; Revelation 20:11-15). Those whose names are written in the book of life will be admitted into heavenly bliss (see Revelation 20:12). At the close of history, God will reward believers for their labors in His kingdom. For unbelievers, the final judgment will seal their eternal doom.

"Peter said, 'Ananias, why has Satan filled your heart to lie to the Holy Spirit and keep back part of the proceeds from the field? Wasn't it yours while you possessed it? And after it was sold, wasn't it at your disposal? Why is it that you planned this thing in your heart? You have not lied to men but to God!' When he heard these words, Ananias dropped dead, and a great fear came on all who heard. …
"There was an interval of about three hours; then his wife came in, not knowing what had happened. 'Tell me,' Peter asked her, 'did you sell the field for this price?'
'Yes,' she said, 'for that price.'
"Then Peter said to her, 'Why did you agree to test the Spirit of the Lord? The feet of those who have buried your husband are at the door, and they will carry you out!' Instantly she dropped dead at his feet. … Then great fear came on the whole church and on all who heard these things."
Acts 5:1–11

"For we must all appear before the judgment seat of Christ, so that each may be repaid for what he has done in the body, whether good or bad."
2 Corinthians 5:10

Beside the following statements, write *D* for discipline, *J* for judgment, and a *FJ* for final judgment.

_____ Its purpose is to make people more like Christ.

_____ When this occurs, there is no more possibility of reform or returning to God.

_____ This is evidence that you are a child of God.

_____ This can serve as a deterrent to sin for others.

_____ This can be applied to believers as well as unbelievers.

_____ This occurs only for unbelievers.

_____ This can be used to vindicate God's holy name.

God deals with sin in three ways: discipline, judgment, and final judgment.

God deals with sin in three ways: discipline, judgment, and final judgment. Discipline comes as the loving response of a Father who wants to help His children know how they are to live. Judgment is for those who reject God's directives. Final judgment is for those who never yield their life to Christ's lordship. Our earnest prayer is that individuals and churches will turn to God before He must bring judgment on them.

Responding to God in Prayer

Psalm 139:23-24 says,

> *"Search me, God, and know my heart;*
> *test me and know my concerns.*
> *See if there is any offensive way in me;*
> *lead me in the everlasting way."*

Ask God, as the psalmist did, to search your heart to reveal anything that is displeasing to Him. Ask God to help you hate sin in your life as much as He does. If the Holy Spirit brings anything to your attention, take time to thoroughly deal with that sin. Confess it; turn from it; and if necessary, make amends and restitution for it.

Day 3 The Means of God's Discipline and Judgment

Disobedience and a Tornado

During King Ahab's reign over Israel, his corrupt wife Jezebel promoted the worship of Baal—the god of the storm. Worshippers believed Baal was responsible for bringing rain, crucial for the success and prosperity of this agrarian nation. Farmers would pay homage to Baal in hopes that he would send rain which would enable bumper crops. God responded to this apostasy by disciplining His people. He sent a drought that lasted three years (1 Kings 17:1). God's people had abandoned Him to follow a non-existent god because they wanted rain on demand. So, God shut up the heavens to demonstrate that He alone controlled nature. For three years the priests of Baal conducted worship services and offered sacrifices, but they could not conjure even a dew drop. When the country reached desperate conditions, God's prophet Elijah called a meeting of King Ahab and all the priests of Baal on Mount Carmel. If God not withheld the rain, no one would have listened to Elijah. But the drought got people's attention and proved to the nation that there is one true God. The Bible tells of numerous occasions where God used nature to regain His people's devotion.

Examples of God's Discipline and Judgment

Many people, even Christians, are squeamish about attributing to God any natural disaster that destroys people. But the Bible describes numerous occasions when God marshaled the forces of nature to gain people's attention and at times to bring judgment on them.

The means God uses to discipline His people can often be quite similar to the means He uses to bring judgment. The primary difference lies in the severity. For example, a storm that causes financial hardship could be a form of discipline. A storm that causes death and widespread suffering would be a form of judgment. Scripture makes it clear that God uses tragedies to reprimand His people (see Deuteronomy 27; 28:15-67; 2 Chronicles 6). These include:

- Natural disaster: earthquake, volcano, hurricane, tornado, flood, fire, drought, hail, famine, insect plague, attack of wild animals
- Disease: plague, wasting disease, fever, leprosy
- Human conflict: war, attack by an enemy, being taken into captivity, bloodshed, increase in wickedness, broken relationships, economic collapse

Although God uses natural disasters as a means of His discipline and judgment, not every crisis is necessarily God's judgment. Scripture indicates that this world is decaying and under the curse of sin (see Romans 8:18-22). Disease and the effects of aging are inevitable because we inhabit imperfect, earthly bodies. Storms occur because of the way nature functions. Nevertheless, when disasters or conflicts occur, God's people should seek to understand if God is communicating His displeasure.

Sometimes when God judges groups such as churches or nations, seemingly innocent people are hurt. God's judgments do not affect only the wicked. Sin's tragedy is that it harms innocent as well as guilty people. But none of us are completely innocent. All have sinned (see Romans 3:23). When Adam and Eve rejected God's command, countless people through the ages suffered as a consequence. When God judged Judah during Ezekiel's day, He said,

> "Since I will cut off both the righteous and the wicked, My sword will therefore come out of its sheath against everyone from the south to the north. So all the people will know that I, the Lord, have taken My sword from its sheath—it will not be sheathed again. But you, son of man, groan! Groan bitterly with a broken heart right before their eyes." Ezekiel 21:4–6

"I consider that the sufferings of this present time are not worth comparing with the glory that is going to be revealed to us. For the creation eagerly waits with anticipation for God's sons to be revealed. For the creation was subjected to futility—not willingly, but because of Him who subjected it—in the hope that the creation itself will also be set free from the bondage of corruption into the glorious freedom of God's children. For we know that the whole creation has been groaning together with labor pains until now."
Romans 8:18-22

When you read that God uses natural disasters as a means of judgment, do you view these verses as merely Old Testament examples, or do you think this happens today? What are some modern natural disasters that may have been instruments of divine judgment?

Why do you think God allows innocent people to suffer along with the wicked when He brings judgment on people?

Expressions of God's Judgment

Although God is unwavering in His response to sin, He also deals with us uniquely and individually. The Bible relates a number of ways God disciplined individuals and nations. If people respond with hearts ready to repent when convicted by the Holy Spirit, God does not discipline them further. But when people refuse to turn from their sin, God applies discipline with increasing severity. The following are methods God may use to discipline His people.

1. God may refuse to hear their prayers.

Silence is one of God's ways to gain people's attention. God does not promise to always answer our prayers. Isaiah 59:2 says,

> *"Your iniquities have built barriers*
> *between you and your God,*
> *and your sins have made Him hide His face from you*
> *so that He does not listen."*

When we sense God is not hearing our prayers, it is imperative that we quickly find out why.

2. God may hide His presence from us.

> *"LORD, how long will You continually forget me?*
> *How long will You hide Your face from me?"* Psalm 13:1

Of David's anguished pleas with God after he sinned, his most heartwrenching cry was in Psalm 51:11,

> *"Do not banish me from Your presence*
> *or take Your Holy Spirit from me."*

There can be no greater punishment than separation from God. The very essence of hell is the complete absence of God's presence. Although it is true that God is omnipresent (see Psalm 139:7-16), He can turn His face from us so that we no longer feel His nearness. Read Isaiah 59:1-3 in the margin.

In times of revival, people report that God seemed to come near to His people. Tragically, it can take a long time before some churches or individuals realize they have moved far from God. A heartbreaking account of God's withdrawing from His people is found in the Book of Ezekiel. God gave the prophet a vision, allowing him to observe the gradual withdrawal of God's presence from His people. First God left the holy of holies, which was the traditional place of His presence. Then He moved to the threshold of the temple (see Ezekiel 10:4). Later God's Spirit moved to the east gate of the temple (see Ezekiel 11:1). Finally, the Lord departed to the Mount of Olives outside the city (see Ezekiel 11:23). Rabbinic tradition claimed that God's presence remained on the Mount of Olives for three and a half years waiting to see whether His people would repent. But they did not. It seems incredible that God's presence could leave the temple and even the city without His people noticing. But when enemies surrounded the city and threatened its destruction, the people cried out to God only to discover He was no longer there. Perhaps that is the imagery intended in the Book of Revelation when the risen Christ declared He stood at the door of His church and knocked, waiting to see whether people would realize He was standing outside and would open the door to let Him in (see Revelation 3:20).

God can gradually remove His presence from your life if you are unwilling to repent. What are some warning signs indicating that God's presence is being removed from our lives?

3. God may withhold speaking to His people.
The Old Testament prophet Amos said,
> *"Hear this! The days are coming—*
> *this is the declaration of the LORD God—*
> *when I will send a famine through the land:*
> *not a famine of bread or a thirst for water,*
> *but of hearing the words of the LORD.*
> *People will stagger from sea to sea*
> *and roam from north to east,*
> *seeking the word of the LORD,*
> *but they will not find it."* Amos 8:11-12

God's word brings life (see Deuteronomy 8:3). The absence of His guidance and communication is evidence of His displeasure. Throughout history revivals erupted when a preacher spoke who had a word from the Lord. People realized they had not been hearing from God; when they did, great conviction of sin resulted. The ministries of revival preachers such as George Whitefield and D. L. Moody attest to what God will do when He has willing servants to deliver His Word in a day of spiritual apathy. These men would readily acknowledge it was not their preaching

"Indeed, the LORD's hand is not too short to save, and His ear is not too deaf to hear. But your iniquities have built barriers between you and your God, and your sins have made Him hide His face from you so that He does not listen. For your hands are defiled with blood, and your fingers with iniquity; your lips have spoken lies, and you mutter injustice."
Isaiah 59:1-3

"He humbled you by letting you go hungry; then He gave you manna to eat, which you and your fathers had not known, so that you might learn that man does not live on bread alone but on every word that comes from the mouth of the LORD."
Deuteronomy 8:3

skill that brought spiritual renewal. Rather, people knew they had just heard from God and were compelled to repent.

4. God may remove the wall of protection from us and those we love.

As believers, we should completely trust God for our protection. But if we have sinned, then we should not expect for God to continue His watchcare of our lives.

> *"I will tell you*
> *what I am about to do to My vineyard:*
> *I will remove its hedge,*
> *and it will be consumed;*
> *I will tear down its wall,*
> *and it will be trampled.*
> *I will make it a wasteland.*
> *It will not be pruned or weeded;*
> *thorns and briers will grow up.*
> *I will also give orders to the clouds*
> *that rain should not fall on it."* Isaiah 5:5-6

God does not cause every bad thing that happens to people who sin. However, all God must do is remove His protective care from His people for natural disasters and evil people to do their worst. God's people usually take His care over them for granted until He withdraws it. When God allows tragedy to strike His people, they must seek to understand why the Lord at least temporarily removes His hand of protection from them.

5. God may allow us to face the full consequences of our own sinful behavior.

The Bible describes how the Lord allows people to reap what they have sown:

> *"God delivered them over in the cravings of their hearts to sexual impurity, so that their bodies were degraded among themselves. ... God delivered them over to degrading passions. ... God delivered them over to a worthless mind to do what is morally wrong. They are filled with all unrighteousness, evil, greed, and wickedness. They are full of envy, murder, disputes, deceit, and malice. They are gossips, slanderers, God-haters, arrogant, proud, boastful, inventors of evil, disobedient to parents, undiscerning, untrustworthy, unloving, and unmerciful."* Romans 1:24-31

Sin is its own worst punishment, guaranteeing innumerable painful results.

Sin is its own worst punishment, guaranteeing innumerable painful results. When someone commits adultery, that sin carries inevitable disastrous consequences: alienation from children, family, friends, church members; feelings of guilt, anger and remorse; loss of position and respect; and financial hardships. God's Word warns that every sin ushers in its own aftermath of strife and suffering (see Romans 6:23).

6. Ultimately, God may choose to destroy or bring down those who refuse to repent.

> *"Your enemies will build an embankment against you, surround you, and hem you in on every side. They will crush you and your children within you to the ground, and they will not leave one stone on another in you, because you did not recognize the time of your visitation."* Luke 19:43-44

God has never hesitated to use ungodly instruments to punish His people. God used the wicked Assyrians to punish the northern kingdom of Israel. He used King Nebuchadnezzar to overthrow Jerusalem. God later allowed the Roman legions to decimate the temple. It is foolish for God's people to assume He will always protect them from their enemies regardless of how they live. As the writer of Hebrews gravely warned, "It is a terrifying thing to fall into the hands of the living God!" (10:31).

> **Have you experienced or witnessed any of these judgments? If so, describe what happened.**

If we refuse to repent when God calls us back to Him, He will eventually deal decisively with our stubbornness. He will not wait indefinitely as we continue to blatantly defy Him. If we persist in our resistance, He will bring judgment on us. The New Testament gives several examples when this type of judgment happened.

The Destruction of Jerusalem

Jesus had prophesied the destruction of Jerusalem that eventually took place in A.D. 70. It was a judgment on the Jewish people for rejecting Him as God's Messiah (see Luke 19:41-44).

The Corinthian Christians

Paul rebuked the Corinthian church for not taking the Lord's Supper seriously. They were sinning against Jesus' body and blood and then hypocritically partaking of the Lord's Supper as if their hearts were pure before God. Paul warned:

> *"Whoever eats and drinks without recognizing the body, eats and drinks judgment on himself. This is why many are sick and ill among you, and many have fallen asleep. If we were properly evaluating ourselves, we would not be judged, but when we are judged, we are disciplined by the Lord, so that we may not be condemned by the world."* 1 Corinthians 11:29-32

Apparently, some church members actually died because they refused to conduct themselves properly during that sacred observance.

> *"The wages of sin is death, but the gift of God is eternal life in Christ Jesus our Lord."*
> *Romans 6:23*

The Ephesian Church

The risen Christ warned of impending judgment of the church in Ephesus when he said in Revelation 2:5, "Repent, and do the works you did at first. Otherwise, I will come to you and remove your lampstand from its place—unless you repent."

> **Do you think the modern church is concerned about God's judgment? What is the evidence for your answer?**

> **Are there signs that modern society is already under God's judgment? If so, what is the evidence?**

Some people have developed a false theology that they believe releases them from any personal accountability for sin once they are saved. They argue that God does not punish those who are redeemed and are covered by Jesus' blood. They suggest that when God looks at them, He sees only Jesus. Two of the preceding New Testament examples involved Christians and churches. Jesus has indeed paid the penalty for all sin—past, present, and future—so that our eternal destiny is firmly secured when we are born again. However, our relationship with Him and our usefulness to His kingdom purposes can be greatly hindered by our sin.

God is not more lenient with the sin committed by Christians than He is with the sin of unbelievers. Sin is sin. In fact, He is more relentless at rooting sin out of the lives of Christians. Paul taught this lesson to the Roman believers:

> *"What should we say then? Should we continue in sin in order that grace may multiply? Absolutely not! How can we who died to sin still live in it? ... We know that our old self was crucified with him in order that sin's dominion over the body may be abolished, so that we may no longer be enslaved to sin, since a person who has died is freed from sin's claims."*
> Romans 6:1-7

Sin robs Christians of abundant life and tarnishes the reputation of Christ. Having been freed from sin's claim for condemnation, we should rejoice in God's vigilant care to keep us separated from sin's consequences in this life and in eternity.

Responding to God in Prayer

Have you been treating sin in your life lightly? Reflect on any difficult events you have recently experienced. Could any of these trials be God's discipline or judgment? Why might God be allowing these circumstances? What might He be doing in your life? Pray and ask God to open your spiritual understanding to every adjustment He requires in your life. Then be prepared to respond in obedience.

Day 4 Spiritual Warfare and God's Discipline

Spiritual Attacks

Henry was once visiting a town in northern Canada where his church and its missions team were preparing to plant a new church. Suddenly the witch doctor from the local native community stepped into the street near Henry and called for everyone's attention. He informed everyone that he was placing a curse on Henry for starting a church in the community. This man began calling on evil spirits to oppose the proposed mission. In the following weeks many spiritual battles were fought as a Christian witness was extended into that community.

Scripture warns, "Our battle is not against flesh and blood, but against the rulers, against the authorities, against the world powers of this darkness, against the spiritual forces of evil in the heavens" (Ephesians 6:12). The apostle Peter also wrote of the dangerous nature of our adversary. Read 1 Peter 5:8-9 in the margin.

He taught that the devil is like a lion on the hunt seeking to destroy us (see 1 Peter 5:8). Nevertheless, Satan's power to harm God's people is much less potent than God's capacity to bring judgment on His wayward people. While Scripture exhorts Christians to resist the devil, we are also commanded to fear the Lord (Psalm 19:9; 34:9; 111:10; Matthew 10:28; 1 Peter 2:17). Therefore, it would be foolish to attribute God's discipline to Satan's attacks. God's people must learn to discern the difference.

> *"Be sober! Be on the alert! Your adversary the Devil is prowling around like a roaring lion, looking for anyone he can devour. Resist him, firm in the faith, knowing that the same sufferings are being experienced by your brothers in the world."*
> *1 Peter 5:8-9*

Spiritual Warfare

Spiritual warfare is initiated by Satan and his evil forces for the purpose of thwarting God's work. God deals with us in truth (see John 14:6), but Satan mobilizes lies against us (see John 8:44). The purpose of spiritual warfare is to discourage us and to fill us with guilt and fear. The forces of wickedness will try to make us focus on ourselves and our inadequacy rather than on Christ and His sufficiency. When trying to discern whether the adversity you are facing is the discipline of God or the attacks of spiritual warfare, ask these questions:

- 🐦 Is this teaching me to be humble or causing me to be proud?
- 🐦 Is it encouraging me to be Christlike or self-centered?
- 🐦 Is it causing me to trust in the Lord or to struggle with doubt?
- 🐦 Is it setting me free from sin or making me feel guilty?
- 🐦 Am I being drawn to pray or tempted to be self-reliant?

When God revives His people, Satan vehemently opposes that work. Paul wrote in Ephesians 6:10-17 that Christians must be prepared for assaults from the spiritual forces of darkness. Nevertheless, it is foolish to attribute every difficult experience to Satan's attacks. When a pastor has a cold and cannot preach on Sunday, it is possible

> *"You are of your father the Devil, and you want to carry out your father's desires. He was a murderer from the beginning and has not stood in the truth, because there is no truth in him. When he tells a lie, he speaks from his own nature, because he is a liar and the father of liars."*
> *John 8:44*

that he simply caught a virus. Life has setbacks. Cars break down, and the economy fluctuates. Not every negative event is an attack from Satan. However, Scripture is clear that God allows and uses bad circumstances to discipline His people. It would be futile if every time God disciplined you, you assumed it was spiritual warfare, with Satan orchestrating events. If, rather than seeking what God is saying to you through your trying circumstances, you cry out to God for protection from Satan's ploys, you are missing the point of God's discipline.

Satan and his minions seek to hinder you from serving and glorifying the Lord. God's discipline, on the other hand, is designed to remove anything from your life that is not Christlike. If, for instance, God wants to build patience in your life, He may allow you to encounter trying circumstances so that you have the opportunity to learn patience. This is not spiritual warfare. It is God using ordinary experiences to help you become more like Jesus. If you resist this work and cry out to God for deliverance, you may miss God's purifying activity in your life. When hardships come, always ask: Is this an ordinary life experience that comes to every person who lives in a decaying body and a sin-filled world? Is God using these events in my life as a means of pruning me so that I become more like Christ? Or is my condition an expression of spiritual warfare designed to distract me or prevent me from glorifying God?

> **List characteristics of spiritual warfare in the left column and characteristics of God's discipline in the right column.**
> ### *Spiritual Warfare*　　　　*God's Discipline*

Are you presently going through a difficult time? Are the pressures you are enduring drawing you closer to Christ or further from Him?

At the end of Jesus' ministry, He warned Simon Peter of an impending spiritual attack he was to endure. Jesus described it as being sifted like wheat in Luke 22:31. In the face of this spiritual attack, Jesus assures Peter that He has prayed for him and instructs Peter to strengthen his fellow believers once restoration comes to him personally. Jesus is more aware of the spiritual warfare than we could ever be. In fact, He intercedes for us before we even know the attack is coming and is ready to restore us in the event that we fall into temptation. Once again, God's love shines through the darkness of even Satan's vicious attacks upon the church.

Principles of God's Judgment

As we have seen, God passes judgment on Christians as well as unbelievers. He decisively deals with those who refuse to turn from their sin or whose actions could encourage others to sin. As we examine God's methods of judgment, several scriptural truths are important to reiterate and understand.

Judgment begins with God's people:

First Peter 4:17 says, "The time has come for judgment to begin with God's household; and if it begins with us, what will the outcome be for those who disobey the gospel of God?" Although Christians are exempt from condemnation, they are the first to receive judgment in this life.

Every deed will be judged:

"God will bring every act to judgment, including every hidden thing, whether good or evil" (Ecclesiastes 12:14). We should live with the understanding that we cannot hide our sin any more than a preschoolers can hide their rebellion from their parents.

Jesus came to bring judgment:

John 9:39 states, "Jesus said, 'I came into this world for judgment, in order that those who do not see will see and those who do see will become blind.'" God is so serious regarding judgment of sin that it stands as one reason for Christ's arrival on earth.

God's judgments are always right, true, and fair:

It is said of God in Revelation 16:7, "Yes, Lord God, the Almighty, true and righteous are Your judgments." Such a declaration can be made because of God's perfect character. We do not have to second-guess His intention or His decisions.

> **Why do you think God begins judgment with His own people?**

> **Ecclesiastes 12:14 says, "God will bring every act to judgment, including every hidden thing, whether good or evil." What concerns does this raise about how you are living?**

God's discipline is generally progressive. Although sometimes, such as in the case of Ananias and Sapphira, judgment is immediate, it usually comes after a period of increasingly severe discipline. Each time we do not respond to God, His action becomes more intense. Read Leviticus 26:14-33 in the margin as an illustration.

Did you notice the increasing severity of God's responses to rebellion? God generally does not begin by dispensing His most devastating punishments. However, if we do not return to Him after His mild discipline, He increases its severity until we can ignore Him no longer.

> **Name a difficult circumstance you experienced that was a result of living in an evil, decaying world.**

"If you do not obey Me and observe all these commands ... I will do this to you. ... If after these things you will not obey Me, I will proceed to discipline you seven times for your sins. I will break down your strong pride. ... If you act with hostility toward Me and are unwilling to obey Me, I will multiply your plagues seven times for your sins. ... If in spite of these things you do not accept My discipline, but act with hostility toward Me, then I will act with hostility toward you; I also will strike you seven times for your sins. ... And if in spite of this you do not obey Me but act with hostility toward Me, I will act with furious hostility toward you; I will also discipline you seven times for your sins. ... I will destroy. ... I will reduce your cities to ruins ... I also will devastate the land. ... I will scatter you among the nations."
Leviticus 26:14-33

Name a circumstance you experienced that may have been the result of spiritual warfare.

Name a circumstance in your life that may have been God's discipline.

Reflect on these events to observe how they are similar and how they are distinct in what they produced in your life.

In the sinful and temporary world in which we live, we face numerous painful experiences. One reason is that this earth is not our home. Our bodies are deteriorating, and we share the planet with evil people who bring calamity on others. Our world is also a battleground on which Satan and his forces fight a desperate, losing battle against God's kingdom. Though he has been fatally wounded, he is still mortally dangerous and hates God's people. The greatest reality of our world, however, is that God rules over it. It is His activity and not Satan's that should occupy our attention. Christians should seek to discern among natural circumstances, spiritual warfare, and God's discipline and judgment so that we can respond appropriately.

Responding to God in Prayer

Can you discern the difference among natural calamities, spiritual warfare, and God's discipline? Ask God to open your spiritual understanding so that you gain His perspective on what you are experiencing. If it is a normal difficulty that people typically experience, ask God to give you His strength, wisdom, and peace to endure it. If it is spiritual warfare, ask God to aid you in firmly putting on the spiritual armor required to resist it (see Ephesians 6:10-17). If it is God's discipline, pray that He will grant you a sensitive heart to immediately and wholeheartedly yield to His discipline and return to God with all your heart.

Day 5 Responding to God's Discipline

Fatherly Discipline

Henry and his wife, Marilynn, reared five children, and each one responded differently to parental discipline. One grimly faced chastisement and refused to yield an inch. Another argued and sought to have the charges reduced. Another ingeniously invented ways to make himself immune to the punishment he received. The fourth child began weeping and repented before any consequences had even been handed out. Their youngest child and only daughter watched the misery her older brothers faced and decided it didn't pay to disobey!

As each child misbehaved, each one received discipline. Each responded uniquely. So it is with God's children. The way we respond to God's discipline determines the measure of our spiritual growth. Just as the condition of our hearts determines how we respond to a word from God, the condition of our hearts affects how receptive we are to God's discipline. Jesus uses a parable in Matthew 13 to show that the same seed (His Word) can be planted in different types of soils (dispositions of our hearts) and can produce varied results.

As a child, how quickly did you respond to your parents' discipline?

As a believer, what has been your response to receiving God's discipline? Have you appreciated it or resented it?

Has God's chastisement made you more like Christ or bitter about frustrating circumstances in life? Why?

God Measures His Discipline to Our Hearts

God is a loving Father who does not delight in the suffering of His children. But He knows that sin brings death, and if left unchecked, sin will destroy His children. Therefore, God does whatever is necessary to turn us away from sin. Because God is motivated by perfect love, He does not discipline us any more severely than is necessary to bring about spiritual growth and maturity.

A 17th-century Puritan pastor named Henry Scougal observed, "God hath several ways of dealing with the souls of men, and it sufficeth if the work be accomplished, whatever the methods have been."[2] God perfectly measures His discipline to our heart's condition. Some people's hearts are so hard that only major discipline will humble them. For others, the slightest expression of disapproval from God is sufficient to drive them to their knees.

A 19th-century English pastor named Octavius Winslow described God as "a tender, loving father; so tender and so loving, that not one stroke, nor one cross, nor one trial more does he lay upon us, than is absolutely needful for our good;—not a single ingredient does he put in our bitter cup, that is not essential to the perfection of the remedy."[3] Winslow cited Peter's example when he denied his friendship with Jesus on the night of the crucifixion. Such a shameful act deserved Jesus' most bitter rebuke.

God perfectly measures His discipline to our heart's condition.

Jesus might have publicly berated His disloyal disciple or demoted him to minor assignments in His kingdom. But Jesus, in His grace, knew all that was required for His zealous, overconfident disciple: Jesus merely glanced at Peter (see Luke 22:61). That one gentle look crushed Peter's tender heart. He immediately realized the awful thing he had done. That one gaze from Jesus devastated Peter, and he went out into the night and wept bitterly (see Luke 22:62). We should all strive for hearts so receptive toward God that only a glance in our direction was needed for us to grieve over any offense we had committed against our beloved Savior!

How has God's discipline in your life been perfectly suited to bringing you to repentance?

What level of discipline is required to send you humbly to your knees? Put a mark next to your level of sensitivity to God's discipline.

[ ] **Retain a hardened heart**
[ ] **Become angry**
[ ] **Resent discipline**
[ ] **Argue with God**
[ ] **Respond half the time**
[ ] **Eventually come around**
[ ] **Am generally receptive**
[ ] **Become heartbroken that discipline was necessary**

What relationship do you think exists between your acceptance of God's discipline and the spiritual growth you have experienced in your life?

If there is such an instance, describe a time in your life when your acceptance of God's discipline contributed to your spiritual growth

Restoration

Peter obviously had a tender heart toward His Lord. When he realized the grievous thing he had done, he went out and wept bitterly. But what did Jesus do with His wayward disciple next? In that famous encounter by the seashore after His resurrection, Jesus took Peter aside to talk with him (see John 21:15-19). What must Peter have thought was coming? Would Jesus verbally berate him? Would Jesus list the consequences Peter would suffer for his failure?

What did Jesus do? There was no tongue-lashing from Jesus. He did not publicly humiliate Peter. At this moment Jesus sought to restore Peter to the love relationship begun three years earlier. Jesus did not ask Peter for a confession of sin but for a confession of love. At the root of Peter's failure was a love problem. Jesus intended to bring Peter back into a love relationship with Himself. God never disciplines us out of anger or vengeance. He disciplines us to restore us. That is an important difference between spiritual warfare and God's discipline. When God's chastisement has done its work, our relationship with God is closer than before.

> **What strikes you about the way God restores people after He has disciplined them?**

> **How is God's discipline different from what many earthly parents do when disciplining their children?**

Perhaps your family was not a place where love was expressed well. Maybe it was not expressed at all by your parents. You face a unique temptation to allow the negative memories from childhood to color your current relationship with your Heavenly Father, especially of His discipline. If your personal family history is marked by unpleasant memories, take some time today to talk to your Heavenly Father about it. Now is the time for you to allow God to eradicate any bitterness you hold toward family members and any distance in your relationship with Him due to your past experiences. Use Romans 8:12-16 and 1 John 3:1-3 as a guide for your conversation with God in prayer.

God does not discipline us from anger or spite but always from love. His discipline is always for a purpose: to restore our fellowship with Him. The key to the intensity of God's discipline lies with us. If our hearts are tender toward Him and quick to respond to His activity in our lives, all we may require to repent is His mournful gaze. But if we harden our hearts and try to justify our wrongdoing, God's discipline will grow increasingly severe. It is always tragic to resist the loving parental overtures of our loving Heavenly Father.

Responding to God in Prayer

Take a moment to reflect on your heart's sensitivity toward God. Have you required only a look from Jesus for your heart to melt over your sin? Or have you stubbornly denied any wrongdoing? Has God had to bring severe punishment on you before you yielded to His work in your life? Take time to pray and ask God to make your heart so sensitive to Him that you quickly respond to anything He wants to do in your life. Then immediately respond in obedience.

1. Abraham Lincoln, "Proclamation of a National Fast Day," *The Collected Works of Abraham Lincoln* (New Jersey: Rutgers University Press, 1953), 4:482.
2. Henry Scougal, *The Life of God in the Soul of Man* (Philadelphia: Westminister Press, n.d.), 69.
3. Octavius Winslow, *Personal Declension and Revival of Religion in the Soul* (Pennsylvania: The Banner of Truth Trust, 1978), 176.

"When they had eaten breakfast, Jesus asked Simon Peter, 'Simon, son of John, do you love Me more than these?' 'Yes, Lord,' he said to Him, 'You know that I love You.' 'Feed My lambs,' He told him. A second time He asked him, 'Simon, son of John, do you love Me?' 'Yes, Lord,' he said to Him, 'You know that I love You.' 'Shepherd My sheep,' He told him. He asked him the third time, 'Simon, son of John, do you love Me?' Peter was grieved that He asked him the third time, 'Do you love Me?' He said, 'Lord, You know everything! You know that I love You.' 'Feed My sheep,' Jesus said. 'I assure you: When you were young, you would tie your belt and walk wherever you wanted. But when you grow old, you will stretch out your hands and someone else will tie you and carry you where you don't want to go.' He said this to signify by what kind of death he would glorify God. After saying this, He told him, 'Follow Me!'"
John 21:15-19

Jesus did not ask Peter for a confession of sin but for a confession of love.

Small Group Discussion Guide

⚛ † ⚛

Open in prayer.

Ahead of time, ask someone to be prepared to pray. Invite prayer requests and ask the group for prayer requests that pertain to personal and corporate revival. Listen for how God is presently working in their lives through the study so that the group will know how to pray for them. Once people have had an opportunity to share, call on the person appointed to pray.

View Session 3 of the Teaching DVD

———— *Truths to Remember*

———— *Scriptures to Read*

———— *Quotes to Remember*

———— *Actions to Take*

If you missed this session, go to *www.lifeway.com/freshencounter* to download this and any other session of *Fresh Encounter.*

Discussion Guide

Ask what group members have learned about the heart this week. Take 5 to 10 minutes for individuals to share what God taught them through the study.

Could you identify with the material from your own experience?

Can you give any examples of how you have seen churches disciplined by God?

Ask members to share their reactions to the DVD segment.

Read Hebrews 12:7-11 and answer the following questions.

How could the relationship with our earthly father affect our view of God?

Discuss how God's care of our lives is superior to any earthly parent.

What are the primary reasons for which God disciplines His people?

Discuss the different methods which God uses to discipline His people. Refer back to pages 69-75 to help the group see how God works to discipline His people.

How did God describe His discipline of the Israelites in Isaiah 5:2-5?

Regarding God's discipline, Richard said on the DVD, "God has a way of raising His voice in your life." Ask for someone to share how they have experienced God's discipline in their lives; especially how God used increasingly difficult circumstances to alert them of their sin.

Using James 4:8, the Blackabys encouraged us to respond to God's discipline by "returning to the point of departure."

How can a Christian discern where that departure point was?

What should we do once we have identified it?

Discuss the differences between God's discipline, spiritual warfare, and the natural circumstances of a fallen world.

Where do you see God's discipline active at the moment? It might be in the nation, on a church, or in your own life.

Take time to honestly discuss how God is working specifically in your life to call you to a more faithful relationship with Christ.

Close in prayer.

UNIT 4: REPENTANCE: RETURNING TO GOD

Scripture-Memory Verse

"'Return to Me, and I will return to you,' says the LORD of Hosts."
MALACHI 3:7

Unit Overview

DAY 1: GOD'S REMEDY FOR SIN

DAY 2: TURNING BACK TO GOD

DAY 3: CHARACTERISTICS OF TRUE REPENTANCE

DAY 4: CORPORATE REPENTANCE

DAY 5: SPIRITUAL AWAKENING

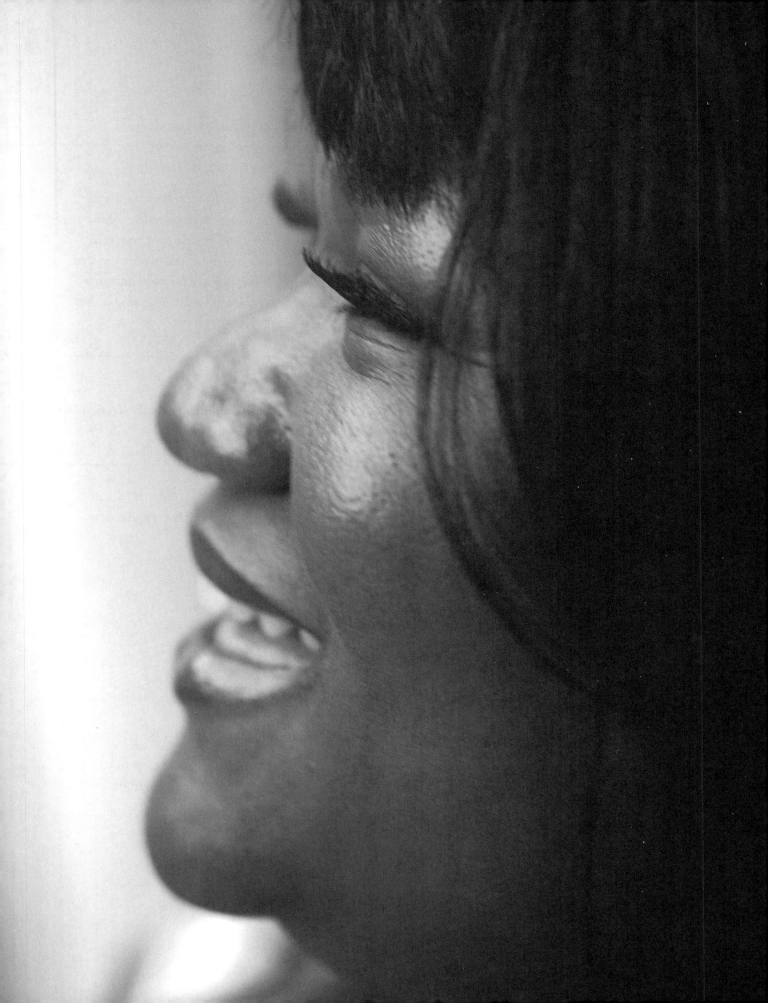

Cleansing by Washing with Water Through the Word

THIS WEEK WE WILL LEARN ABOUT REPENTANCE. It is often perceived as one of the most negative words in the Bible. Perhaps that is because we desire to set our own course and be the master of our own lives. But we will find that repentance is a vital part of the process in being revived as believers and experiencing revival in our churches. Once again, we turn to Ephesians 5 to reiterate Christ's intention is to present us in purity so that we will be radiant in His sight: *"Christ loved the church and gave Himself for her, to make her holy, cleansing her in the washing of water by the word. He did this to present the church to Himself in splendor, without spot or wrinkle or any such thing, but holy and blameless"* (Ephesians 5:25-27).

Wash Out

Are there actions, behaviors, habits, or sins that need to be cleansed from your life, family, or church? Confess these sins (agree with God about the wrongdoing), turn away from them, and turn to God.

Soak In

Are there good things that need to be absorbed into your life and relationships? Pray about those and seek to become all God wants you to be.

→ **1 John 1:9-10**

→ **Proverbs 11:19**

→ **2 Corinthians 6:14-17**

→ **Jeremiah 6:15**

→ **Jeremiah 17:14**

→ **Ezekiel 18:30-32**

→ **Hebrews 12:1-2**

→ **Ezekiel 36:26**

Keep the verses above in mind as you work through the Bible studies this week. Use the space below to keep a list of the specific lessons you learn from your studies and how God is applying these lessons to your life.

Experiencing God's power
Revival in Tennessee

On October 20, 2006, pastor Mark Partin led his church in LaFollette, Tennessee, to begin a series of revival meetings with Mark Douglas preaching. The meetings lasted 40 days. At the close of the first service, one young woman came forward to pray during the altar call. In the evening service, the tide of revival came in. This is how pastor Partin described it: "We faithfully returned for Sunday-evening service. After singing only two songs, God began blowing His sweet breath throughout the congregation. His presence became so strong and real. Streams of people began flowing from their seats directly to the altar. They begged for the opportunity to confess sin. No one had even been asked to confess sin. The Word of God had not even been preached. But God was extending the offer for His people to come before Him, to purify themselves, to be cleansed, to be set free. People were responding."

Douglas preached each evening for two weeks before returning to his own church. Partin took over the preaching and later wrote these words: "Night after night people continued to confess their sins. Following the delivery of God's Word and message, complete silence would fall upon the congregation like a veil. Amazingly, in spite of so many people being present, not a sound could be heard ... no rustling of papers, no movement of bodies shifting, not even the sighs of people breathing ... nothing! And then breaking through the silence you would hear footsteps. Footsteps that clicked with force and determination to reach the altar, footsteps that were driven by purpose, footsteps that were being guided by the hand of God."[1]

Many sins were confessed during the services. Women admitted to conceiving children out of wedlock. Men confessed to forcing women to have abortions. A man wept because God had called him into ministry when he was 19, but he had disobeyed. People confessed adultery, addictions, greed, bitterness, and unforgiving hearts in services lasting three to four hours. People felt convicted over sins they had committed decades earlier. Individuals suddenly found themselves at the altar without any recollection of deciding to go forward. Each morning when the church doors opened at eight o'clock, people were waiting to enter the auditorium to pray.

Two things characterized this divine movement. First was an overwhelming sense of God's presence. The people attending the services knew they were encountering God. They entered the auditorium anticipating that God would meet them. Second, there was profound conviction of sin. When God visits His people, His power is palpable, and an uncovering of our sinfulness is inescapable.

✵ † ✵

Day 1 ## God's Remedy for Sin

Repentance in Brownwood

In February 1995, Henry Blackaby was speaking at a series of meetings at Howard Payne University and Coggin Avenue Baptist Church in Brownwood, Texas. On January 22, the Holy Spirit began to work powerfully among the people of Coggin Avenue. While Henry was on the Howard Payne campus, God continued the work He had begun. During a luncheon for businesspeople, although no invitation had been extended, a man suddenly stood up and publicly confessed that he needed to be made right with God. Then, as Henry led a meeting for students that evening, two male students ran to the platform and announced that God had been convicting them of their sin and that they could find no peace until they publicly confessed their wrongdoing. Henry gave them the microphone, and the two young men tearfully confessed their sin.

Then Henry asked whether, in light of what had just been shared, other men needed to repent of their sins as well. Many students rushed to the front. Two female students approached the microphone and confessed that they too needed to repent of the way they had been living. When Henry asked whether other female students needed to repent, many crowded to the front asking for God's forgiveness. The time of repenting continued late into the night. Students from that campus went to other colleges to share what had happened, and revival broke out on other campuses as well.

God Brings His People Back to Himself

Richard Owen Roberts notes that the message of revival is the message of repentance.[2] When we depart from our relationship with the Lord, He lovingly disciplines us. We need to make the connection between our sin and what is happening to us. If we are experiencing God's discipline, we must immediately respond. The longer we delay, the harder our hearts will become. When we cry out to Him for relief from our sin and its consequences, He invites us to repent and return to Him: " 'Return to Me, and I will return to you,' says the LORD of Hosts" (Malachi 3:7).

Describe the feelings you associate with repentance.

Repentance is one of the most positive words in the Christian vocabulary. It is God's remedy for sin. Every person has sinned (see Romans 3:23). Sin's penalty is spiritual death (see Romans 6:23). If not for God's provision of repentance, our sin would forever condemn us to separation from God and bondage to sinful habits. But God promises that if we confess our sin and return to Him, He will forgive our sin and set us free to experience the abundant life He intends for us (see 1 John 1:9).

"All have sinned and fall short of the glory of God."
Romans 3:23

Repentance is one of the most positive words in the Christian vocabulary.

"The wages of sin is death, but the gift of God is eternal life in Christ Jesus our Lord."
Romans 6:23

Read 1 John 1:9 in the margin. Confession is a key component of repentance, but we sometimes hesitate to confess our sins to God. Place a check mark beside each reason you sometimes hesitate to confess your sins.

[ ] I'm embarrassed by what I have done.
[ ] I've confessed it so many times before.
[ ] I'm not sure God will forgive me again.
[ ] I feel too hopeless.
[ ] I'm not sure I will ever truly change.

King Solomon understood that God's people would inevitably sin and depart from Him. As he dedicated the temple in Jerusalem, he asked God if He would forgive His people when they cried out to Him. Take a moment and read Solomon's prayer in 2 Chronicles 6:24-39 to understand the heart of repentance.

All sin is ultimately against God. Solomon knew God could use drought, famine, plague, insects, military defeat, and captivity to discipline His people. His question was: Lord, if You punish Your people because of their sin and they turn their hearts back to You, will You forgive them?

God's Promise for Revival

God answered with a resounding yes! Read 2 Chronicles 7:13-14 in the margin. If He punished His people for their sin and they returned to Him, He would forgive and restore them. In His reply to Solomon, God identified four requirements for revival: humility, prayer, seeking God, and repentance leading to a change in behavior. When God's people fulfill these requirements, God responds by forgiving their sin and blessing the land.

How often do you repent of your sin?

[ ] Never
[ ] Once when I became a Christian
[ ] Rarely
[ ] Periodically
[ ] Daily

How often do you think a person should confess sin?

Has repentance become a lifestyle for you, or is it something you do only when the pressure of your sin becomes too much to bear?

"If we confess our sins, He is faithful and righteous to forgive us our sins and to cleanse us from all unrighteousness."
1 John 1:9

All sin is ultimately against God.

"If I close the sky so there is no rain, or if I command the grasshopper to consume the land, or if I send pestilence on My people, and My people who are called by My name humble themselves, pray and seek My face, and turn from their evil ways, then I will hear from heaven, forgive their sin, and heal their land."
2 Chronicles 7:13-14

You may assume only major sins need to be confessed. Many consider ungodly habits such as telling white lies or blurting out profanities or unkind words in a moment of anger too common to bother confessing. We can excuse such sins by saying, "Well, that's just the way I am," "Everyone has his weaknesses," or "God knows I don't mean anything by it." Yet the closer we draw to God, the more grievous our seemingly minor sins appear. Every sin is an offense against Almighty God. Even supposedly harmless transgressions can lead to spiritual death for those outside of faith in Christ. The frequency and earnestness of your confession and repentance reveal your sensitivity to God and your awareness of the costliness of your sin.

What are some sins in your life that you have tended to treat as minor or insignificant?

How do you sense God wants you to adjust your attitude toward them?

Encountering God in Prayer

Ask God to help you view the sin in your life the same way He sees it. Ask Him to make you aware of sins you have not treated seriously. Take time to confess those to God and repent of them. Ask God to sensitize your heart to the seemingly smallest offense against your holy, loving Savior.

Day 2 Turning Back to God

In an earlier week, I told you the story of how God used Marie Monsen to incite a revival among missionaries in China. Remember the three questions she asked:
1. Have you been born of the Spirit?
2. What evidence do you have of the new birth?
3. Have you been filled by the Holy Spirit?

C. L. Culpepper, a respected missionary leader testified to his experience under the Holy Spirit's conviction to these questions: "The Holy Spirit and God's Word continued to probe until I believed I would die under the searching, accusing finger of God. ... I told my Chinese co-workers that in their compliments of me as an effective worker I had stolen God's glory. My heart was so broken I didn't believe I could live any longer."[3] Once God cleanses His people from their sin, He can use them in a mighty revival.

How seriously do you view sin in your life?

[   ]   I try to deal with the really big sins of my life.
[   ]   If God draws my attention to a sin, I eventually repent of it.
[   ]   When my sin begins to cause problems in my life, I address it.
[   ]   I regularly search my life for anything that displeases God.
[   ]   I have grown to hate sin and quickly repent of any sin I commit.

In times of revival, people come under a tremendous sense of conviction. They may spend hours confessing their sins until late into the night because they cannot bear to ignore them any longer. When the Holy Spirit begins to work among people, He brings to mind sins that used to seem inconsequential or reminds them of transgressions committed years previously that continue to weigh on their souls.

Symptoms of Spiritual Illness

Repentance is God's cure for sin. Sin is the symptom of a heart that has departed from God. Just as a cardiologist would look for particular physical manifestations to detect heart disease, certain clues reveal whether our hearts have departed from God. The following are three characteristics of spiritual sickness that requires repentance.

1. Undergoing God's discipline.

If we are under God's discipline, it indicates a sin problem. God will discipline us in many different ways. He may refuse to give us spiritual victories, withhold His blessing, or remove His protection from our lives. For example, Scripture warns husbands that God doesn't listen to the prayers of a man who mistreats his wife (see 1 Peter 3:7). We must readily recognize God's hand of discipline so that we can quickly repent of any sin that is hindering our walk with Him.

2. Turning to or accepting substitutes for God's presence, purposes, or ways.

Who or what we turn to first in times of difficulty reveals where we have placed our trust. If in an economic downturn we immediately call our boss, accountant, or financial adviser instead of turning to God in prayer, we reveal we are not trusting the Lord. When substitutes for God appear in our lives, it is time to repent.

3. Disobedience to the clear will of God as revealed in His Word.

In times of revival, people often confess they have known what God wanted them to do but have refused to obey. God told them to forgive someone, report dishonesty in their business dealings, apologize to someone they had offended, go on a mission trip, or enter full-time Christian ministry, but they resisted. When we are running from God, the rationalizations for our disobedience can seem reasonable to us. But when the Holy Spirit shines His penetrating light on us, we recognize our sin as blatant rebellion against our Creator, and we are compelled to repent.

Reflect on the three previous indicators of sin. If one or more of these are present in your life, take a few moments in prayer right now to seek God in repentance.

What actions (such as devotional practices) could you begin that would aid your relationship with Christ in such a way that you could avoid a lifestyle of sin?

Unconfessed sins are evidence that a person has abandoned a love relationship with the Father. Nancy Leigh DeMoss notes, "When we cease to sense the seriousness of our sin, we also cease to be moved by the wonder of Christ's sacrifice on the cross for sin."[4] Whenever we recognize the symptoms of spiritual illness in our lives, family, church, denomination, or nation, we need to cry out to God for deliverance. We cannot cure ourselves or others of sin. We can beseech the Lord to intervene. The good news is that God is fully prepared to help us. In fact, by the time we call out to Him, He already has everything prepared for revival. God gave the people this amazing promise when He led Israel into captivity because of its sin:

> *"This is what the Lord of Hosts, the God of Israel, says to all the exiles I deported from Jerusalem to Babylon: 'For I know the plans I have for you'—this is the Lord's declaration—'plans for your welfare, not for disaster, to give you a future and a hope. You will call to Me and come and pray to Me, and I will listen to you. You will seek Me and find Me when you search for Me with all your heart. I will be found by you'—the Lord's declaration—'and I will restore your fortunes and gather you from all the nations and places where I banished you'—the Lord's declaration. 'I will restore you to the place I deported you from.'"*
>
> Jeremiah 29:4,11-14

Underline each phrase in the previous passage that indicates what God wants to do for His people if they repent.

How do these verses make you feel about the issue of repentance?

Even while His people were languishing under the consequences of their sin, God had everything in place to draw them back to Himself. He was prepared to bless them. He was only waiting for their prayerful, repentant cry. When they began to seek Him, He was ready to respond. Today is no different for God. For today's church to be revived, all they must do is seek His presence once again. Just as in the days of Jeremiah, the Lord has a great future and hope awaiting His people if they will only cry out to Him.

By the time we call out to Him, He already has everything prepared for revival.

Encountering God in Prayer

Is there an attitude or a behavior in your life that is separating you from God? Do you sense God drawing you back into a loving, obedient relationship with Him? Take time in prayer to identify anything about your life that could be displeasing to God. Decide that you will not walk in rebellion when you could walk closely with Christ.

Day 3 Characteristics of True Repentance

Amazing Grace

Henry and Richard were traveling across America conducting a series of meetings. In each place the worship leader inevitably led the congregation in singing the classic hymn "Amazing Grace" by John Newton. The lyrics include the phrase that God "saved a wretch like me." After one service a man approached them, obviously agitated. He said he used to be a pastor but had "fallen into an affair." His wife had divorced him, and his church had dismissed him as pastor. He went on to recount his disappointment in his denomination and its leaders, whom he had considered to be his friends. Although he believed God had forgiven him of his sin, he complained that denominational leaders were refusing to help him find a new pastorate. He noted that Christians were the most unforgiving people he knew. His bitterness at his perceived mistreatment was quite evident.

Not long after that, Henry and Richard were ministering inside Angola State Prison in Louisiana, which houses thousands of inmates serving life sentences. The inmates also sang "Amazing Grace." These men, however, sang those words with conviction. They knew they had been wretches! But there in prison, serving life sentences, they had found Christ. They knew they were sinners, but ironically, in prison they were set free by God. Several inmates declared that going to prison was the best thing that had happened to them because there they had finally met God. It was impossible to listen to hundreds of inmates, wearing prison garb and singing in unison, "My chains are gone; I've been set free" without being moved to tears.

How would you account for the different ways the former pastor and the inmates dealt with their sin?

What tempts you to react as the former pastor did to the consequences of sinful decisions?

"Amazing Grace"

Amazing grace how sweet the sound
That saved a wretch like me
I once was lost but now I'm found
Was blind but now I see

'Twas grace that taught my heart to fear
And grace my fears relieved
How precious did that grace appear
The hour I first believed

My chains are gone I've been set free
My God my Savior has ransomed me
And like a flood His mercy reigns
Unending love, amazing grace

The Lord has promised good to me
His word my hope secures
He will my shield and portion be
As long as life endures

My chains are gone I've been set free
My God my Savior has ransomed me
And like a flood His mercy reigns
Unending love, amazing grace

The earth shall soon dissolve like snow
The sun forbear to shine
But God who called me here below
Will be forever mine ...
You are forever mine[5]

Repentance involves more than merely acknowledging the sin; that is confession. We have known many people who were caught committing a sin such as embezzlement or adultery. Once exposed, they acknowledged what others now knew. Yet some stubborn souls seemed to resent that there were consequences for their sin. They correctly believed that because God had forgiven them, people should too. However, forgiveness does not exempt people from consequences or future accountability.

The pastor who committed adultery firmly believed he should be immediately welcomed back into the pastorate. His sense of entitlement did not demonstrate genuine repentance. He was oblivious to the devastation his sin had caused others and the dishonor his actions had brought to God's name. When this man sang the lyrics of "Amazing Grace," he did not recognize what a wretch he truly was. Moreover, this man mistakenly assumed that because he confessed his sin, God had automatically forgiven him. God does not forgive us because we speak words of confession. According to 2 Chronicles 7:14, He forgives us when we humble ourselves, turn from our sin, and seek His face. We will know God has accepted our repentance when we sense He has drawn near to us once again. As James 4:8 says, "Draw near to God, and He will draw near to you."

The inmates in that maximum-security prison had no doubt they were wretched sinners before they met Christ. Those who shared their stories did not rail against the injustice of their imprisonment. Did they long to undo the consequences of their sin? Yes. But they had truly repented. They made no demands on God or anyone else. They understood that experiencing God's grace was a matter of relationship, not circumstances or location.

What image comes to mind to describe how offensive our sin is to God?

What changes in a person show evidence that a person recognizes the offensiveness of sin and has genuinely repented?

A Call to Repent

God calls His people to repent or perish. Sin is lethal, and we must treat it as such. Jeremiah described the nation's spiritual condition during his time. The people were steeped in sinful depravity, but the leaders were unconcerned about the evil that pervaded society. No one grasped the danger of the wicked practices of the day—not even the priests or prophets:

> "From the least to the greatest of them,
> everyone is gaining profit unjustly.
> From prophet to priest,
> everyone deals falsely.
> The have treated My people's brokenness superficially,

Sin is lethal, and we must treat it as such.

claiming: Peace, peace,
when there is no peace.
Were they ashamed when they acted so abhorrently?
They weren't at all ashamed.
They can no longer feel humiliation.
Therefore, they will fall among the fallen.
When I punish them, they will collapse,
says the LORD.
This is what the LORD says:
Stand by the roadways and look.
Ask about the ancient paths:
Which is the way to what is good?
Then take it
and find rest for yourselves.
But they protested: We won't!" Jeremiah 6:13-16

Then, as now, genuine repentance was scarce. Repentance is not merely being sorry you got caught or even remorse about your sin. The motivation to repent is not primarily to avoid God's wrath. The Puritan pastor, Henry Scougal noted: "Repentance itself is a delightful exercise when it floweth from the principle of love."[6]

Remorse is inadequate. Behavior modification is ineffectual. Returning to religious activity is futile. Confession is part of repentance in that we acknowledge our wrongdoing, but repentance also involves a broken heart and a decisive return to God. Repentance without absolute humility is not repentance at all; it is at best rededication. "Godly grief produces a repentance not to be regretted and leading to salvation, but worldly grief produces death" (2 Corinthians 7:10).

Repentance also involves a broken heart and a decisive return to God.

> **Underline acts of genuine repentance.**
> Acknowledging your wrongdoing once you have been caught
> Admitting wrongdoing but resisting the consequences
> Humbly accepting any consequences for sin
> Brokenhearted over offending God
> Arguing with God about the seriousness of your offense
> Claiming the past is the past

God wants us to love Him with our entire being. When we return to our love relationship with Him, our lifestyle reflects the transformation. As the last prophet to prepare the way for Jesus' coming, John the Baptist called not just for a turning from sin but also for a lifestyle that reflected inner change: "He [John the Baptist] went into all the vicinity of the Jordan, preaching a baptism of repentance for the forgiveness of sins. He then said to the crowds who came out to be baptized by him, 'Brood of vipers! Who warned you to flee from the coming wrath? Therefore produce fruit consistent with repentance'" (Luke 3:3,7-8).

What are some positive changes that have been produced in your character when you intentionally repented and turned from sin?

New life in Christ reflects repentance. Paul wrote in Galatians 2:19-20, "I have been crucified with Christ; and I no longer live, but Christ lives in me. The life I now live in the flesh, I live by faith in the Son of God, who loved me and gave Himself for me." The evidence of repentance is that once again, Christ freely lives His life in and through you.

A Personal Journey

Repentance for God's people—as individuals or as a church—involves a threefold process of change.

1. An adjustment of attitude.

"For I am conscious of my rebellion, and my sin is always before me. Against You—You alone—I have sinned and done this evil in your sight. So You are right when You pass sentence; You are blameless when You judge."
Psalm 51:3-4

A change of mind is required in which we agree with God about the truth of our sin. This is confession. We affirm that what we have done is wrong. If we argue with God about whether we have sinned, we are not in a position to repent! If we make excuses for our behavior or are upset at the consequences of our sin, we are unprepared for repentance. Like King David, we must come to a place of conscious admission of our sin. Read Psalm 51:3-4 in the margin.

2. A change of heart.

Instead of reveling in our sinful ways, we must grieve over our sin as the Father does. If our transgression does not break our hearts, we make a mockery of Christ's supreme sacrifice on the cross. David said,

> *"The sacrifice pleasing to God is a broken spirit.*
> *God, You will not despise a broken and humbled heart."* Psalm 51:17

"I have this against you: you have abandoned the love you had at first."
Revelation 2:4

Alienation from God begins when we lose sight of our first love (see Revelation 2:4). Only after we have returned to loving the Lord can we willingly obey Him. A change of heart is prerequisite to lasting obedience.

3. Transformed desires and actions.

Too many Christians attempt to walk as close to the world as possible without sinning. We flirt with temptation when we should flee from it. Repentance requires intentional living. We must rid ourselves of any idol of the heart and tear down the strongholds that keep us from holiness. We must remove ourselves from tempting situations. These actions require a change of the will. Simply saying you are sorry is inadequate. We change our very desires.

Give one example of how you have flirted with temptation and another example of how you could have fled from it.

> **Flirted:**

> **Fled:**

If you desire to change your will, God will enable you to do so, "for it is God who is working in you, enabling you both to will and to act for His good purpose" (Philippians 2:13). Once you have asked God to change your heart, you must allow Him to transform your actions as well.

> **Suppose a friend came to you and told you he knew he had been sinning and wanted to turn his life around. How would you advise him? What steps would he need to take?**

Encountering God in Prayer

Pause and recall the sins you committed during the past week. Did you repent of them? How do you know whether your repentance was acceptable to God? Ask God to show you how to repent in a way He finds acceptable. Draw near to God and watch for Him to draw near to you (James 4:8).

Day 4 Corporate Repentance

A Prayerless Church

In April 1994 a small rural church in Tennessee met for a special emphasis on prayer. Following the study, members were asked to share what God had taught them. The pastor stood and confessed, "I have not been a man of prayer, and I have not led you to be a people of prayer. I need to ask you to forgive me."

The conference leader asked the pastor to pray aloud, confessing his sin to the Lord and seeking His forgiveness. Then the church members expressed their forgiveness to their pastor. Eager to get right with the Lord, they joined their hearts and voices in prayers of confession. Together the congregation repented of their sin of neglecting to pray. Their pastor led in a prayer of confession. He begged God to make them a prayerful congregation. Then the people spread out across the worship center to pray in small groups.

God did a special work of grace in that church. Following that collective encounter with Him, the people began to take prayer much more seriously. Their personal prayer lives were rejuvenated. They scheduled time for prayer in Bible study gatherings and worship times. They regularly called special prayer meetings. During this time their pastor felt led by God to resign, and the congregation made prayer a major element in seeking a new pastor.

In the spring of 1995 the church called a new pastor on whom God had already placed a burden for prayer. God's powerful presence became increasingly evident as prayer permeated the congregation. Inactive church members returned. Members decisively dealt with sin. People in the community were drawn to the church, and numerous nonbelievers chose to put their faith in Christ. What had begun with one man's confession of sin grew to transform an entire congregation and the surrounding community. What a beautiful picture of how repentance can change a church and city!

One person can have a profound effect when he or she chooses to follow God. Who is an individual whom God has used to lead you toward repentance? Describe how God used this person in your life.

Corporate Sin

Just as individuals sin, so do corporate bodies such as families, churches, denominations, and nations. At times people may assume that they can anonymously sin within the context of a group setting. For example, an individual Christian might recognize the sinfulness of acting in a racist way toward a colleague at work, yet she might condone or ignore racist policies at her church or in her community. Or while an individual might know it is wrong to disobey when God speaks to him, he might readily vote with the faction of his congregation that opposes stepping out in faith as God is leading the church. When a group sins, that group is accountable to God to repent.

At times a family, church, or nation may refuse to repent. As years go by, the generation that sinned may no longer be present, yet the consequences of the sin remain. For example, a church might callously dismiss their pastor with trumped-up charges, treating him and his family harshly and unfairly. Or the church might have undergone a bitter split in which a large number of members were acrimoniously expelled. In both cases time may have passed, but the church has never accepted responsibility for the unchristian way it behaved. Even though the people directly involved may no longer attend, God may still hold the church accountable for its sin and refuse to bless it. In such cases the current members and leaders need to understand corporate repentance.

Whenever people sin, repentance is required. This includes not only individuals but also—

> ❧ Families that sin;
> ❧ Committees that sin;
> ❧ Churches that sin;
> ❧ Cities that sin;

When a group sins, that group is accountable to God to repent.

- ꝰ Businesses that sin;
- ꝰ Nations that sin;
- ꝰ Denominations that sin.

Choose three of the previous categories and write a sin beside each that the group could possibly commit.

Sin is an affront to Holy God. God's opinion matters infinitely more than people's. Read what God said to His people through the prophet Ezekiel in the margin.

The way God's people act reflects on His holy name. God is jealous for the glory of His name before a world that watches His people. He will not allow His people to dishonor Him with impunity. When church members want to leave their sins in the past or start over, this does not satisfy God's requirements for repentance. God condemned Judah's spiritual leaders because they treated His people's sins so lightly (see Jeremiah 6:14). We cannot merely move on or cover our sin. Sometimes churches try to hide members' transgressions because they are concerned about the church's reputation in the community. Unfortunately, such churches may be more concerned with a community's opinion than they are with God's.

What are some barriers that discourage a church or another group of believers from collectively repenting of sin?

Churches must repent of their corporate sins much as individuals do. Without repentance, fellowship with God will remain broken.

Read from the Book of Revelation the following messages the risen Christ delivered to five different churches and record the sins Christ called for them to repent of.

Ephesus in 2:4-5:

Pergamum in 2:14-16:

Thyatira in 2:20:

Sardis in 3:1-3:

Laodicea in 3:15-16:

The five churches in Revelation were called to repent. Sin committed by a group is still sin. Churches may adopt policies and promote activities that are unbiblical. Members may form splinter groups and act in an ungodly manner. Factions can meet to slander and oppose the pastor. Financial leaders can use unethical means to accomplish church goals. Church leaders can manipulate people to serve. Staff can be unfairly

> *" 'Then I had concern for My holy name, which the house of Israel profaned among the nations where they went. Therefore, say to the house of Israel: This is what the Lord God says: It is not for your sake that I will act, house of Israel, but for My holy name, which you profaned among the nations where you went. I will honor the holiness of My great name, which has been profaned among the nations—the name you have profaned among them. The nations will know that I am Yahweh'—the declaration of the Lord God—'when I demonstrate My holiness through you in their sight.' "*
> *Ezekiel 36:21-23*

> *"They have treated My people's brokenness superficially, claiming: Peace, peace, when there is no peace."*
> *Jeremiah 6:14*

fired. Gossip and slander can run rampant through the congregation. When a church sins, every member must assume a portion of the guilt. At times, however, church members assume that because they did not directly commit the transgression, they are not responsible. The refusal to repent can be devastating to churches.

What corporate sins do you see in your—

Family?

Church?

Denomination?

Nation?

What role could you have to encourage corporate repentance?

How does a church or a religious group repent? Second Chronicles 7:14 outlines God's provision for corporate repentance. Before revival comes, God's people must first humble themselves. Pride is the first and greatest barrier to revival. Because of pride, churches may be reluctant to admit any wrongdoing. The thought of publicly repenting is repugnant to them. How does God respond when His people try to hide their sin? He tells us,

> *"The one who conceals his sins*
> *will not prosper,*
> *but whoever confesses and renounces them*
> *will find mercy."* Proverbs 28:13

Congregations, Christian organizations, and families must learn to renounce their pride and humble themselves before God. In order to do so, our pride must be set aside so we can hear God's clear call to faithfulness.

After humility comes prayer—communicating with God and seeking His face. Hiding from God is impossible. Trying to avoid Him or run from Him is futile. Running to our God is the only remedy for our wretched condition. God said to Judah,

> *"Come, let us discuss this. ...*
> *Though your sins are like scarlet,*
> *they will be as white as snow;*
> *though they are as reed as crimson,*
> *they will be like wool."* Isaiah 1:18

Running to our God is the only remedy for our wretched condition.

When we humbly seek God's presence, we are in a position to repent. Then we must turn from our wickedness. Repentance, as we have already studied, requires a change in mind, heart, will, and actions. It results in a changed lifestyle. Like an individual, a repentant church must turn away from its sin. This may require tearing down idols, changing the way services and meetings are conducted, getting rid of traditions, selling property, disbanding particular committees, or making restitution for wrongs committed. Saying, "We'll try to do better next time" is insufficient. Repentance requires actions in the present, not just a promise for the future.

The Joy of Repentance

A few years ago a congregation was faced with a sensitive but not uncommon situation. An unmarried couple in the church, new believers, had been living together, and it became obvious they were expecting a child. Extenuating circumstances had prevented them from marrying as soon as they became believers. The woman was separated from a husband who had been abusive and unfaithful but who had refused to grant a divorce. The man was from another country and could not obtain employment until his immigration papers arrived.

Nonetheless, the pastor and deacons helped the couple recognize their situation dishonored God and the church. The couple tearfully repented, and the deacons immediately helped them pay for separate housing. That same week every obstacle to their marriage was suddenly removed. On Sunday this man and woman stood before their church family and humbly confessed their sin. They desired to be married immediately. The congregation's response was overwhelming. Members flew into action cooking, baking, and decorating; and that afternoon the church gathered again to celebrate a wedding. This dear couple and their children remain a cherished and vibrant part of that church fellowship. Repentance is to be embraced as the most positive response believers can have to God's work.

Rather than ignoring members' obvious sins, church leaders must firmly and lovingly address the situation and provide assistance to help them do what honors God. New believers should be able to count on their church leaders to help them know how to live godly lives. When churches refuse to address sin in the lives of their members, they are corporately responsible for it. Clearly, repentance opens the door to forgiveness, fellowship, and joy, not just for the penitent ones but for the entire Christian community. According to Acts 3:19, repentance is God's provision to bring us back into the abundant life He longs for us to enjoy.

> Reflect on the church that confronted the couple in the previous example. Do you think church leaders handled the situation biblically?

> Why do so few churches confront sin this way?

Repentance requires actions in the present, not just a promise for the future.

Repentance is to be embraced as the most positive response believers can have to God's work.

"Repent and turn back, that your sins may be wiped out so that seasons of refreshing may come from the presence of the Lord."
Acts 3:19

What are reasons a church might avoid addressing such situations?

Encountering God in Prayer

Spend time praying for the various groups to which you belong: family, church, business, denomination, nation. Are there sins you have condoned simply by your reluctance to speak up? If so, pray for God to move in your midst to draw His people under conviction to repentance. Ask God to use your life in His plan to draw people back to Him.

Day 5 Spiritual Awakening

Our Need for Awakening

The First Great Awakening in America occurred from 1726 to 1755. But by the mid-18th century the movement had subsided, and religious vitality in many parts of the country was decreasing. It has been said that "the last two decades of the eighteenth century were the darkest period, spiritually and morally, in the history of American Christianity, the low watermark of its lowest ebb tide, when infidelity rode roughshod over the feelings of the disoriented majority."[7] For example, by the end of the century, only two students at Princeton University claimed to be religious. The filthy-speech movement was popular among young people, encouraging the use of profane language in public. Devout Christian students in the universities resorted to meeting in secret for fear of being exposed and ridiculed.

But then the Spirit of God began moving across the land as He had in earlier times. Hampton Sydney College, Yale University, Williams College, and others began to see students dramatically revived spiritually. Pastor and evangelist James McGready began to hold communion services for people on the Kentucky frontier, and crowds numbering as many as 25,000 gathered. So many people were being converted that many churches saw their membership reach record levels.

From 1800 to 1830, Presbyterians saw their membership quadruple. Baptists grew in number from approximately 65,00 to more than 517,000. Many new religious mission societies were formed to address needs in the culture. New seminaries were founded to train the large numbers accepting God's call into ministry. Crime rates plummeted, as did occurrences of public drunkenness. As America had been expanding across the continent, it seemed to have lost its moral and spiritual compass. The Second Great Awakening brought thousands of people to faith in Christ and caught the attention of the nation, which had rapidly been drifting away from God.

In week 1 we studied the difference between revivals and spiritual awakenings. In your own words, explain the difference. (Take a look at pages 16-18 if you need a reminder.)

Revival is for God's people. If you have never experienced life, you cannot have your life revived! But once God's people return to Him, we become an instrument He can use mightily to draw unbelievers to Himself in large numbers. A spiritual awakening sweeps across an unbelieving population, changing lives on a large scale and with great speed. When awakenings occur, God does more in a few months than churches and denominations could accomplish over many years.

When awakenings occur, God does more in a few months than churches and denominations could accomplish over many years.

If a spiritual awakening occurred in your city, describe what the effects might be.

Spiritual Awakening at Pentecost

Prior to Jesus' coming, Israel's spiritual condition had dramatically declined. For more than four hundred years, God's people had not heard a word from the Lord through His prophets. The religious group known as the Pharisees formed and developed a legalistic religion based on keeping the letter of the law without considering its spirit. There was no teaching about a personal relationship with the Lord. Temple worship had evolved into a formal ritual rather than a response of the heart. God's people desperately needed revival. But God was watching and the Scripture says, "When the completion of the time came, God sent His Son" (Galatians 4:4). As Jesus first began to preach, His message was simple: "Repent, because the kingdom of heaven has come near!" (Matthew 4:17). Many did repent and return to the Lord. Revival was beginning among God's people.

During the time of Christ's arrest, trial, and crucifixion, His 12 disciples deserted Him. The 40 days between Jesus' resurrection and glorious ascension provided time for renewal of the disciples. The risen Christ used these days to prepare His followers for the amazing works God was going to do through them. "He also presented Himself alive to them by many convincing proofs, appearing to them during 40 days and speaking about the kingdom of God" (Acts 1:3). Jesus pointed His disciples to the Scriptures and explained everything they said about Him. "Beginning with Moses and all the Prophets, He interpreted for them the things concerning Himself in all the Scriptures" (Luke 24:27). The Father was putting everything in place for the imminent outpouring of His Holy Spirit. God's intention was to use a revived people to spiritually awaken the world.

How does your personal willingness to repent of sin affect your ability to obey the Great Commission of Matthew 28:18-20?

When the Holy Spirit came on the day of Pentecost, He empowered the early church to carry out the Great Commission in Matthew 28:18-20. Without a divine assignment there was no need for Pentecost. At this point the disciples had already been revived. Now they were poised for a spiritual awakening that would catapult the church into an international force.

> *"When the day of Pentecost had arrived, they were all together in one place. Suddenly a sound like that of a violent rushing wind came from heaven, and it filled the whole house where they were staying. ... Then they were all filled with the Holy Spirit and began to speak in different languages, as the Spirit gave them ability for speech. There were Jews living in Jerusalem, devout men from every nation under heaven. When this sound occurred, the multitude came together and was confused because each one heard them speaking in his own language. And they were astounded and amazed, saying, 'Look, aren't all these who are speaking Galileans? How is it that we hear, each of us, in our own native language? ... We hear them speaking in our own languages the magnificent acts of God.' And they were astounded and perplexed, saying to one another, 'What could this be?'"* Acts 2:1-12

When God's people fully surrender, God will draw the world to Himself through His people. Peter addressed the inquisitive crowd by preaching from the Scriptures about the coming of the Holy Spirit. He then proclaimed Jesus as the Savior.

> *"'Let all the house of Israel know with certainty that God has made this Jesus, whom you crucified, both Lord and Messiah!' When they heard this, they were pierced to the heart and said to Peter and the rest of the apostles: 'Brothers, what must we do?' 'Repent,' Peter said to them, 'and be baptized, each of you, in the name of Jesus the Messiah for the forgiveness of your sins, and you will receive the gift of the Holy Spirit.' ... Those who accepted his message were baptized, and that day about 3,000 people were added to them."* Acts 2:36-41

Peter's message, though brief, was from God; so the results had God-sized dimensions. This biblical account is a clear example of what God will do in a spiritual awakening when His people are fully surrendered to Him. On this occasion God displayed His power through the believers as they spoke foreign languages they had not learned. Then after a brief message, thousands were deeply convicted by the Holy Spirit to repent and be baptized. The church began with 120 believers, and God added 3,000 in a single day. That is spiritual awakening!

Think about the requests you normally make to God and take this simple inventory.

Do I pray regularly for God to bring about revival and spiritual awakening?   Yes   No

Do I ask for God-sized results from my requests?   Yes   No

Do I truly believe God can act miraculously in my church and community?   Yes   No

Moving from Revival to Awakening

This is God's pattern—revival among God's people and then spiritual awakening among unbelievers. The people were filled with awe as they witnessed God's miraculous work. Their lives were changed. They lived unselfishly with joyful and sincere hearts. They enjoyed favor in the eyes of the public. This is the kind of church that draws unbelievers to Christ! The close relationship these early Christians enjoyed with the Father bound them together in love, and their Christlike love for one another attracted many others to join them. The Book of Acts records how the spiritual awakening continued:

"Many of those who heard the message believed, and the number of the men came to about 5,000." Acts 4:4

"Believers were added to the Lord in increasing numbers—crowds of both men and women." Acts 5:14

"The preaching about God flourished, the number of the disciples in Jerusalem multiplied greatly, and a large group of priests became obedient to the faith." Acts 6:7

"The church throughout all Judea, Galilee, and Samaria had peace, being built up and walking in the fear of the Lord and in the encouragement of the Holy Spirit, and it increased in numbers." Acts 9:31

"This became known throughout all Joppa, and many believed in the Lord." Acts 9:42

"When the Gentiles heard this, they rejoiced and glorified the message of the Lord, and all who had been appointed to eternal life believed. And the disciples were filled with joy and the Holy Spirit." Acts 13:48,52

This is God's pattern—revival among God's people and then spiritual awakening among unbelievers.

"The churches were strengthened in the faith and were increased in number daily." Acts 16:5

"This became known to everyone who lived in Ephesus, both Jews and Greeks. Then fear fell on all of them, and the name of the Lord Jesus was magnified. And many who had become believers came confessing and disclosing their practices, while many of those who had practiced magic collected their books and burned them in front of everyone. So they calculated their value, and found it to be 50,000 pieces of silver. In this way the Lord's message flourished and prevailed." Acts 19:17-20

As you read these verses describing revival and spiritual awakening, put an *R* beside statements that indicate revival and an *SA* beside comments that indicate spiritual awakening.

Why do you think God brings revival before spiritual awakening?

Today many churches and ministries are committed to evangelism and carrying out the Great Commission. However, just as Jesus' disciples were unprepared to evangelize their world before Pentecost, unrevived church members will be ineffective at evangelizing their world today. However, once the Lord's people return to Him, God brings mighty, sweeping movements of evangelism across a land, wherein thousands and even millions of people enter the churches in a short time span.

Consider the spiritual condition of your nation today. How would a spiritual awakening change the church's frequency, method, and effectiveness in evangelism?

At times human pride convinces believers they can do what only God can do through the working of His Spirit. We are tempted to believe that human planning, administration, marketing, and promotion can accomplish the work of God's kingdom. Today we must humble ourselves and cry out to God to revive us first and then make us instruments in His mighty hand to bring spiritual awakening. Once we see more clearly how He desires to use us then we can be used to make disciples of all nations.

The modern world has millions of people who have never heard the name of Jesus Christ. Many societies oppress their people and inflict grievous suffering on innocent victims. Natural disasters extinguish thousands of lives in a moment. This world needs more than evangelism; it needs a global spiritual awakening. The world cannot be won incrementally. Too many people will enter eternity without Christ if the church continues to reach people one by one. The Spirit of God yearns to gather a massive harvest of souls as He has done in times past. God is not content that anyone should perish.

There has not been a great awakening in America for more than a century. Society continues to deteriorate morally. Crime and violence have escalated. Marriages continue to disintegrate. Suicide is epidemic. God's people must be faithful to witness and teach and minister. But it is incumbent on every believer to pray regularly and fervently that God will send another great awakening that will bring millions of people to Him. The world must be turned back from its impending judgment, and the only way is through the mighty work of the Lord. Christians who have a heart like God must feel compelled to pray every day for God to send another great awakening.

The Spirit of God yearns to gather a massive harvest of souls as He has done in times past.

Encountering God in Prayer

Take time to consider the condition of your city, your nation, and the world. Ask God to lay His heart's desires on your heart. Be a faithful intercessor for your land until God brings an awakening once more. Take time to pray diligently for your church, city, nation, and world. Continue to do so each day until you see God's answer to your prayers.

1. Mark Partin, *The 40-Day Reign of God* (LaFollette, TN: n.p., n.d.), Used by permission.
2. Richard Owen Roberts, *Revival* (Wheaton, IL: Tyndale House Publishers, Inc., 1985), 16–17.
3. C. L. Culpepper, *The Shantung Revival* (n.p., n.d.), 29.
4. Nancy Leigh DeMoss, *Holiness: The Heart God Purifies* (Chicago: Moody Publishers, 2004), 83.
5. John Newton, Louie Giglio, John P. Rees, and Chris Tomlin, "Amazing Grace (My Chains Are Gone)." © Copyright 2002 worshiptogether.com songs/ sixsteps Music (admin. by EMI CMG Publishing). All rights reserved. Used by permission. [online, cited 4 May 2009]. Available from the Internet: *www.lifewayworship.com*.
6. Henry Scougal, *The Life of God in the Soul of Man* (Philadelphia: Westminister Press, n.d.), 56.
7. J. Edwin Orr, *Campus Aflame: A History of Evangelical Awakenings in Collegiate Communities*, ed. Richard Owen Roberts (Wheaton, IL: International Awakening Press, 1994), 33.

Session 4
Small-Group Discussion Guide

꧁ † ꧂

Open in prayer.

Ahead of time, ask someone to be prepared to pray. Invite prayer requests and ask the group for prayer requests that pertain to personal and corporate revival. Listen for how God is presently working in their lives through the study so that the group will know how to pray for them. Once people have had an opportunity to share, call on the person appointed to pray.

View Session 4 of the Teaching DVD

Truths to Remember

Scriptures to Read

Quotes to Remember

Actions to Take

If you missed this session, go to *www.lifeway.com/freshencounter* to download this and any other session of *Fresh Encounter*.

Discussion Guide

Ask members what they learned about repentance this week.

> **In the past, did you view repentance as a positive or negative word?**

> **How do you see it now?**

> **Ask for several people to give their personal definitions of repentance.**

Have the group recite the week's memory verse together.

> **How does the promise in Malachi 3:7 affect the way you view repentance?**

Discuss the three symptoms of spiritual illness listed on page 99.

> **What are some other symptoms in our lives that would lead us toward repentance?**

> **Are any of these symptoms at work in your life currently?**

> **How should we respond if we see these symptoms in the life of another believer?**

The Scripture serves as God's "plumb line" by which we judge our walk with God. What are some biblical passages that you use to measure how well you are following Christ?

Invite sharing about corporate repentance. Discuss how groups such as families or churches can sin and then pass the consequences of the sin down through the next generation.

> **Does anyone presently sense the need for corporate repentance?**

> **What are the indications that our city, state, or nation is in need of a spiritual awakening?**

> **What role would corporate repentance by the church play in God bringing about a spiritual awakening in the culture?**

> **What might spiritual awakening look like if it happened today? Ask participants to share how they are praying for it.**

In the video, Richard referred to the danger of keeping the "communal secret" that we all have sin which needs to be confessed but we continually ignore.

> **How would corporate confession by a church change their ability to obey God and participate in His mission?**

As time allows, call for examples of what God has been doing in group members' lives.

Close in prayer.

UNIT 5: PRAYER AND REVIVAL

Scripture-Memory Verse

"I tell you, all the things you pray and ask for—believe that you have received them, and you will have them."

MARK 11:24

Unit Overview

DAY 1: PRAYING IN FAITH

DAY 2: PRAYING IN RIGHTEOUSNESS

DAY 3: PRAYING WITH PERSEVERANCE

DAY 4: PRAYING CORPORATELY

DAY 5: WATCHMEN ON THE WALLS

Cleansing by Washing with Water Through the Word

PRAYER IS OFTEN SEEN AS A PASSIVE ACTIVITY. Yet, it is one of the greatest methods of participation in God's kingdom. In this week's session, we will study how God desires for His people to actively seek Him through prayer. As God's people cry out in desperation for discernment and humble themselves before God's Word, then they can be directed by God through His Word. Prayer is a powerful gift from Christ who *"loved the church and gave Himself for her, to maker her holy, cleansing her in the washing of water by the word. He did this to present the church to Himself in splendor, without spot or wrinkle or any such thing, but holy and blameless"* (Ephesians 5:25-27).

Wash Out

Are there actions, behaviors, habits, or sins that need to be cleansed from your life, family, or church? Confess them (agree with God about the wrongdoing), turn away from them, and turn to God.

Soak In

Are there good things that need to be absorbed into your life and relationships? Pray about those and seek to become all God wants you to be.

→ **Isaiah 1:15**

→ **Mark 11:22-24**

→ **Mark 9:23-24**

→ **Romans 8:26**

→ **Ephesians 3:20**

→ **Matthew 13:58**

→ **Matthew 7:7**

→ **Matthew 8:13**

Keep the verses above in mind as you work through the Bible studies this week. Use the space below to keep a list of the specific lessons you learn from your studies and how God is applying these lessons to your life.

Experiencing God's power

The Prayer Revival of 1857–58

In 1857 one of the greatest revivals in American history burst forth. The years immediately preceding 1857 saw tremendous growth and prosperity for America. The population was booming and businesses flourished. Materialism captivated the American culture. Simultaneously, churches were declining in numbers, strength, and influence.

In New York City, the swelling population of common laborers in overcrowded tenement buildings forced many wealthy residents out of the downtown area. Most congregations also moved out. But, the North Dutch Church decided to stay and evangelize the surrounding unchurched multitudes.[1] They employed businessman Jeremiah Lanphier as a lay missionary. He was described as "remarkably pleasant, benevolent face; affectionate in his disposition and manner, possessed of indomitable energy and perseverance, having good musical attainments; gifted in prayer and exhortation."[2] He began to visit homes, distribute Bibles, and advertise church services. Facing a discouraging response, he found comfort in prayer.

One day Lanphier earnestly sought the Lord's guidance for how to reach New York City. He sensed God's direction to begin a weekly prayer service for workers and business people during the noon hour. He began on Wednesday, September 23, 1857, with only 6 persons attending. However, it grew each week and their yearning for God became evident. People from every segment of society and every denomination attended the noon prayer meetings.

The devastating financial crash of 1857 hit just weeks after the prayer meetings began. In New York City alone, 30,000 people lost their jobs. In addition to the economic crisis, the nation was gripped by regional tensions over slavery. America's future seemed bleak.

In the midst of these crises, people flooded the prayer meetings by the thousands. Prayer gatherings soon spread throughout New York City and then across the nation. Businesses closed during the noon hour to allow their employees time for prayer. Newspapers devoted front-page coverage to revival news, and revival swept the country.

When the awakening was at its peak, 50,000 people were converted every week. Within a year nearly one million people had been saved. And this growth came from an American population of only 30 million people. Bishop McIlvaine, in his annual address before the Diocesan Convention of Ohio, said, "I rejoice in the decided conviction that it is 'the Lord's doing;' unaccountable by any natural causes, entirely above and beyond what any human device or power could produce; an outpouring of the Spirit of God upon God's people, quickening them to greater earnestness in his service; and upon the unconverted, to make them new creatures in Christ Jesus."[3] J. Edwin Orr, the foremost revival historian of his era, labeled this movement of God "the event of the century."[4] And it all began on the day a humble layman gathered six persons to pray for revival during their lunch hour.

†

Day 1 **Praying in Faith**

Faith at Midnight

DUNCAN CAMPBELL WAS CONDUCTING REVIVAL MEETINGS IN THE SMALL RURAL TOWN OF ARNOL IN THE HEBRIDES ISLANDS OFF THE COAST OF SCOTLAND. The meetings had not begun well, and God's people sensed a breakthrough was needed. One evening several church members gathered with Campbell at the home of Donald and Bella Smith to pray. Sometime after midnight Duncan Campbell asked John Smith to pray. Smith had not yet prayed aloud during the prayer time. After praying for a while, Smith said, "Lord, I do not know how Mr. Campbell or any of these other men stand with you, but I know my own heart, I know that I am thirsty. You have promised to pour water on him that is thirsty. If You don't do it, how can I ever believe You again. Your honour is at stake. You are a covenant-keeping God. Fulfill Your covenant engagement."[5]

As he spoke, the house shook. Many of those inside supposed it to be an earthquake, but later reports confirmed that no one else in the area surrounding the house had felt a tremor. Two persons in that meeting were not Christians and had begun dozing at that late hour. Shaken awake, both placed their faith in Christ for salvation. As the prayer gathering concluded, people left the house only to discover that the entire town had suddenly awakened and many people were silently walking to the church building. Some were carrying chairs and wondering whether there would be adequate room for them. Though the time was past midnight, it was the right time for God to begin the revival in Arnol!

Referring to Smith's prayer, Campbell later exclaimed, "I love to believe that angels and archangels were looking over the battlements of Glory and saying to one another, 'This is a man who believes God!' "[6]

> **From the accounts of Lanphier's prayer meetings in New York City and Campbell's leadership in Scotland, what characteristics do you see as necessary for effective prayer?**

It has been said, "Satan laughs at our toil, mocks at our wisdom, but trembles when we pray."[7] E. M. Bounds wisely stated, "Talking to men for God is a great thing, but talking to God for men is greater still."[8] Studying revivals throughout history reveals that they are not identical. Revivals in Wales, New England, Kentucky, Korea, India, Rwanda, and South Africa all had characteristics that were unique to the people and the social environments in which they occurred. However, in every revival the common denominator is fervent, faithful, persistent, righteous prayer. As Brian Edwards observed, "No church can ever expect revival unless it is praying for it."[9]

However, even though Christians generally recognize the need for prayer, it continues to be one of the most neglected of all Christian practices. Many pastors are faithful to preach on the subject of prayer but few churches are fervently praying. Christians are continually reminded that God has mightily worked in response to His people's fervent praying; yet people still find it difficult to do, or they are unwilling to make prayer a priority. Prayer meetings remain most churches' least-attended gatherings.

Why do you think it is so difficult for people to pray? Check all that apply.

[ ] **Busy schedules**
[ ] **Misplaced priorities**
[ ] **Do not enjoy praying**
[ ] **Unsure of how to pray well**
[ ] **Apathetic**
[ ] **Lack of faith**
[ ] **Unconvinced of the power of prayer**

Revival Praying

Our day calls for people who truly believe that "nothing will be impossible with God" (Luke 1:37). Society not only practices but also flaunts immorality of the lowest nature imaginable. The media mock Christian values. The government legalizes what God condemns in His Word. The majority of today's churches are stagnant or in decline. The number of people who claim to have no religion is rapidly increasing. Apparently, despite state-of-the-art techniques for evangelism, the spread of megachurches, and the proliferation of Christian television, radio, and Internet programs, America continues to spiral downward spiritually. It is an age when concerned Christians must ask, "What can be done?"

Throughout church history numerous revivals and spiritual awakenings have occurred. These divine works have been exceedingly diverse. Some were led by clergy, others by laypersons. Some exhibited dramatic emotionalism, while others were devoid of emotional excesses. Some have lasted for years, others for weeks. Some have been driven by preaching, others by testimonies. As unique as many of these revivals were, one common denominator spanned the centuries: prayer. Even when revivals suddenly burst forth, investigation invariably revealed that people were fervently praying for revival. Matthew Henry declared, "When God intends great mercy for His people, the first thing He does is to set them to praying."[10]

We know that without faith it is impossible to please God (see Hebrews 11:6 in the margin). We may be loyal, orthodox, evangelistic, and missions-minded; but if we lack faith, we cannot please God. Faith goes deeper than desire. As Duncan Campbell explained, "Desire is one thing; confident expectation that the desire will be fulfilled is quite another thing."[11]

"When God intends great mercy for His people, the first thing He does is to set them to praying."
—*Matthew Henry*

"Now without faith it is impossible to please God, for the one who draws near to Him must believe that He exists and rewards those who seek Him."
Hebrews 11:6

How would you characterize the level of faith revealed by your praying? My praying reveals faith that it:

[ ] is growing and deepening;   [ ] is timid;
[ ] is filled with doubts;   [ ] sees miracles;
[ ] does not expect much;   [ ] is only rarely called on;
[ ] has not yet seen all God could do if I truly believed.

William Chambers Burns declared, "The gospel has lost none of its power. It is we Christians who have lost our power with God."[12] He added, "The work of God would flourish by us, if it flourished more richly in us."[13] Throughout history God has moved mightily among His people when they truly believed He would.

While on the earth, Jesus spoke often on the subject of prayer. He taught that faith is an essential component of prayer. Observe what Jesus instructed His disciples about praying in faith:

> *"Jesus replied to them, 'Have faith in God. I assure you: If anyone says to this mountain, "Be lifted up and thrown into the sea," and does not doubt in his heart, but believes that what he says will happen, it will be done for him. Therefore, I tell you, all the things you pray and ask for—believe that you have received them, and you will have them.'"* Mark 11:22-24

Write your own definition of *prayer*.

Prayer is God's invitation for us to come before Him to learn what is on His heart and to respond.

Here is our definition: Prayer is God's invitation for us to come before Him to learn what is on His heart and to respond. Notice that even our prayers are a response to God's work. As with all work in His kingdom, God is the initiator, and we are the respondents. Prayer invites us to delve deeper into our relationship with God so that we can learn what is on God's heart and live according to it. When we come before God with requests, they should be responses to what we are learning from Him. From what we read in Scripture and from what we see in the church today, we should pray in faith for God to send revival to His people.

These times call for mountain-moving prayer!

In times of moral and spiritual decline in society, praying for revival is like asking God to move a mountain. In these times people are no longer interested in biblical spirituality. Even God's people can become so carnal and spiritually lethargic that they see no reason for revival. These times call for mountain-moving prayer!

Perhaps one of the most dramatic examples of praying in faith is the account of the prophet Elijah. Read this familiar story as if for the first time.

> *"Ahab summoned all the Israelites and gathered the prophets at Mount Carmel. Then Elijah approached all the people and said, 'How long will you hesitate between two opinions? If Yahweh is God, follow Him. But if Baal, follow him.' Then Elijah said to all the people, 'Come near me.' So all the people approached him. Then he repaired the LORD's altar that had been*

torn down: Elijah took 12 stones—according to the number of the tribes of the sons of Jacob, to whom the word of the LORD had come, saying, 'Israel will be your name'—and he built an altar with the stones in the name of Yahweh. Then he made a trench around the altar large enough to hold about four gallons. Next, he arranged the wood, cut up the bull, and placed it on the wood. He said, 'Fill four water pots with water and pour it on the offering to be burned and on the wood.' Then he said, 'A second time!' and they did it a second time. And then he said, 'A third time!' and they did it a third time. So the water ran all around the altar; he even filled the trench with water. At the time for offering the evening sacrifice, Elijah the prophet approached the altar and said, 'LORD God of Abraham, Isaac, and Israel, today let it be known that You are God in Israel and I am Your servant, and that at Your word I have done all these things. Answer me, LORD! Answer me so that this people will know that You, Yahweh, are God and that You have turned their hearts back.' Then Yahweh's fire fell and consumed the burnt offering, the wood, the stones, and the dust, and it licked up the water that was in the trench. When all the people saw it, they fell facedown and said, 'Yahweh, He is God! Yahweh, He is God!'"

1 Kings 18:20-21,30-39

What would have happened to Elijah if God had not answered his prayer?

What did Elijah do to demonstrate his confidence that God would answer his prayer?

His simple prayer, devoid of pleading or bargaining, demonstrated a courageous confidence that God would hear him and respond.

Elijah lived in a dangerous, ungodly age. The government leaders were determined to rid the land of its adherence to God, replacing true worship with the abominable idol worship of Baal. Queen Jezebel was a ruthless murderer who would not hesitate to have Elijah cruelly executed. On the mountain 850 antagonistic religious leaders faced down one solitary spokesman for God. Elijah was not merely making a stand of moral conscience; he was putting his life on the line. If God did not respond to his prayer, Elijah was as good as dead. One would think Elijah might have hedged his bets. Perhaps he would have found the driest wood for the altar so that it would easily ignite. He could have chosen to pray at the hottest time of the day. Instead, he doused the wood and the sacrifice with buckets of water and waited until the cool of the day. His simple prayer, devoid of pleading or bargaining, demonstrated a courageous confidence that God would hear him and respond. As a result, heavenly fire fell, and revival burst forth. Elijah didn't hedge his prayers with qualifiers and escape clauses in case God chose not to act. Elijah prayed believing, and the rest is history.

List common hindrances we face that keep us from praying with great confidence.

On this scale how would you rate your faith in prayer?

Doubtful   Confident   Expecting miracles

What has to change in your character or your relationship with Christ to increase the faith in your prayer life?

This is a day that demands Elijah-caliber praying.

Scripture says, "The eyes of the LORD range throughout the earth to show Himself strong for those whose hearts are completely His" (2 Chronicles 16:9). We live in an age that calls for more than timid, cliché-riddled, superficial praying. This is a day that demands Elijah-caliber praying. People who are grieved over the sin and apostasy in their church must cry out to God with bold confidence that God hears them and will respond.

Encountering God in Prayer

Reflect before God on the quality of faith that is evidenced in your prayers. What have you been asking of God that clearly demonstrates to those around you that God is God and there is no other? How are you taking a stand for God through your praying? What mountains are being moved by your prayers?

Day 2 Praying in Righteousness

Crying Out to God

William M'Culloch was a devout pastor in Scotland but not a talented preacher. As a public speaker, he was said to have "virtually no gifts."[14] His voice was reportedly "thin" and "weak," and he was a slow speaker. Those who knew him claimed he was "able, judicious, and faithful, yet no way distinguished as a popular preacher."[15] However, M'Culloch loved his people and had a burning desire to see them experience revival like the ones he read about in America under the leadership of Jonathan Edwards and George Whitefield. Each morning M'Culloch would rise at five o'clock to study for his preaching ministry until eight o'clock in the evening. He faithfully taught God's Word to his people and lovingly ministered to them. But like many pastors before and after him, he was discouraged that Sunday after Sunday the Scriptures seemed to have little impact on his people.

On February 18, 1742, M'Culloch preached on Jeremiah 23:6 in hopes that it would stir the hearts of his people. The passages says, "In His days Judah will be saved, and Israel will dwell securely. This is what He will be named: The LORD Is Our Righteousness." However, as he drew his sermon to a close, the people simply prepared to go home as was their routine. The sight of his flock's continued indifference to God's Word broke M'Culloch's heart. He cried out to God from the pulpit, quoting Isaiah 53:1, "Who hath believed our report, or to whom is the arm of the Lord revealed? Where is the fruit of my labour among this people?"[16] The Holy Spirit brought a powerful sense of conviction on the entire congregation. The auditorium began to reverberate with the sounds of anguished weeping as conviction for sin swept over the people. Daily services ensued and continued for seven months. Every evening the pastor received a steady stream at his home as people sought counsel and received instruction on how to find peace with God. Large crowds began attending the meetings in the town of Cambuslang. Attendance reached 8,000 or 9,000 on a Sunday. M'Culloch invited George Whitefield to preach, and an estimated 20,000 people gathered to hear him at one service.[17]

Despite M'Culloch's efforts to exhort his people, it was his righteous longing, borne from many hours on his knees in private prayer, rather than grand orations from a podium that sparked the outpouring of God's Spirit.

Righteous Praying

Scripture promises that "the intense prayer of the righteous is very powerful" (James 5:16). The righteous prophet Elijah prayed for a drought, and rain did not fall for three years (see 1 Kings 17:1). He prayed again, and fire fell from heaven (see 1 Kings 18:37-38). The prayers of a sanctified prophet were powerful!

James 5:16 reads, "Therefore, confess our sins to one another and pray for one another, so that you may be healed. The intense prayer of the righteous is very powerful." Often Christians latch on to the first part of James 5:16 and only pray with intensity. But the verse qualifies that it is the prayers of a righteous person that God hears. We can be sure that the Lord will listen and respond when we seek to follow Him first with our character and then with our words.

What do you think it means to be righteous as we pray?

Righteousness in prayer means to be right with God, with no sin blocking our prayers from being received by God. Scripture warns,

> "The LORD is far from the wicked,
> but He hears the prayer of the righteous." Proverbs 15:29

No matter how long and hard we plead for revival, if we hold on to our sin, God will not hear our cry. But our hope is found in the converse truth. With Christ in us, we can live righteously and God will hear our prayer. Knowing God's gracious nature, we can rest in the assurance that He will both mold our requests and grant what is best for our lives.

Proverbs warns God's people that the person "who turns his ear away from hearing the law—even his prayer is detestable" (Proverbs 28:9). Righteous praying means asking according to God's nature and Word. That is what praying in Jesus' name implies (see John 14:14). When our heart longs for God's will to be done, He is pleased to give us the desires of our hearts (see Psalm 37:4). Such was the case with the righteous government leader Daniel. Because Daniel's heart was pure before God, God dispatched His answer the moment Daniel prayed. An angel explained to Daniel, "You are treasured by God" (Daniel 9:23). No king or president or prime minister has as much influence on earth as a righteous person who has God's ear.

Consider the condition of your heart when you pray.
Is your heart righteous and blameless before God?   Yes   No
Do you long for God's will to be done?   Yes   No
Do you hate what God despises?   Yes   No
Do you delight when God's will is done?   Yes   No

Now consider God's answers to your prayers.
Do you see God's will being done as you pray?   Yes   No
Does God respond to your prayers?   Yes   No
Is your praying self-centered or God-centered?   Yes   No
Do you seek to adjust God to your will as you pray, or do you adjust your prayers to God's will as you pray?   Yes   No

From the answers you gave, what are the implications to your relationship to Christ?

It is a great challenge for those who pray for revival to remove our wishes and self-interest so that we pray with righteous hearts. Remember the selfish motives of James and John? They asked Jesus if they could sit at His right and left hand when He sat enthroned as the King (see Mark 10:35-37). Clearly, they were not seeking God's will when they made their request. They wanted to manipulate God to suit their ambitions. God does not honor selfish praying, regardless of how much faith we have in making the request. Righteous praying desires God's kingdom to be advanced; it does not seek personal comfort. If God can receive more honor through our suffering than by our comfort, righteous praying will lead us to embrace suffering (see Matthew 26:42; Acts 4:24-31). Righteous praying means we want God's will to be done so much that we are willing to lay our lives on the altar so that we can be a part of God's answer to our prayers.

> *No king or president or prime minister has as much influence on earth as a righteous person who has God's ear.*

It was zeal for God and His people that led Phinehas to take dramatic action against those committing immorality in the Israelite camp (see Numbers 25:1-13). It was love for God and His people that compelled Nehemiah to risk his high position in the king's court in order to see God's people built up. Love for God and His people motivated Queen Esther to risk her life and plead with the king (see Esther 5:1-8). Jeremiah's burden for his people made the prophet cry, "If my head were water, my eyes a fountain of tears, I would weep day and night over the slain of my dear people" (Jeremiah 9:1).

In your community what are the issues to which people give much of their time and energy?

[ ] **Work and business ventures**
[ ] **Cheering on sports teams**
[ ] **Children's activities such as music, dance, or athletics**
[ ] **Involvement in the political process**
[ ] **Religious activities such as church attendance and programs**
[ ] **Hobbies, entertainment, recreation**
[ ] **Spiritual transformation of the city**
[ ] **Community service**
[ ] **Social justice**
[ ] **Fitness**
[ ] **Other:**

How can you be a catalyst for passionate praying in your church for God to bring revival to believers?

The reason some people have a deep longing for revival is that they know what God's judgment and sin's consequences involve. Just as Jesus wept over the city of Jerusalem because He knew it would face certain judgment (see Matthew 23:37-39), those who pray for revival do so because they know certain judgment is coming if God's people do not turn from their sin and return to the Lord. A burden for revival can become all-consuming when you understand what is at stake. Duncan Campbell asked, "We say we want revival, but are we willing to pay the price?"[18] When you have a burden for revival, you will pay any price, rise at any hour, set aside any amusement, and risk misunderstanding from others to plead on your knees for God to revive His people.

Check the statement that best describes the level of urgency with which you pray for revival.

[ ] **Never**
[ ] **Occasionally**
[ ] **Often and intensely**

What comforts, preferences, hobbies, or activities would you eliminate to spend time in prayer pleading for revival?

How do you think God wants your prayer life to change so that you pray in righteousness?

Encountering God in Prayer

Pray as the psalmist did—that God would examine your heart to see if there is any offensive way in you (see Psalm 139:23-24). Ask God to show you your prayers as He views them. Are they self-centered or God-centered? Are you praying with a desperation for revival that God would be pleased to honor? Once you have confessed and repented of your sin, take time to intercede before God with a righteous heart.

Day 3 Praying with Perseverance

Praying Believing

No one in Christian history is better known for his prayer life than George Müller. By faith Müller trusted God for provision for two thousand orphans. He traveled more than 200,000 miles to share the gospel in 42 countries. Yet despite Müller's great faith, God did not always immediately respond to his servant's requests. Müller once said,

> *"In November, 1844, I began to pray for the conversion of five individuals. I prayed every day without a single intermission, whether sick or in health, on the land or on the sea, and whatever the pressure of my engagements might be. Eighteen months elapsed before the first of the five was converted. I thanked God and prayed on for the others. Five years elapsed, and then the second was converted. I thanked God for the second, and prayed on for the other three. Day by day I continued to pray for them, and six years passed before the third was converted. I thanked God for the three, and went on praying for the other two. These two remained unconverted.*
>
> *"The man to whom God in the riches of his grace has given tens of thousands of answers to prayer in the self-same hour or day in which they were offered has been praying day by day for nearly thirty-six years for the conversion of these individuals, and yet they remain unconverted. But I hope in God, I pray on, and look yet for the answer. They are not converted yet, but they will be."[29]*

It was not until after Müller's death that the final man for whom he had prayed would be converted. But just as Müller believed, the man was saved.

At times we demonstrate our faith in God and His providence by praying and believing God will answer soon. At other times we demonstrate our faith by continuing to pray over a long period of time, expecting that one day we will indeed receive His answer even though it has not yet come.

List the three things you have been praying for longest. Beside each one mark the scale to indicate your level of confidence in God's eventual answer.

Request	My Confidence in God's Answer
1. _____	1 2 3 4 5 6 7 8 9 10
2. _____	1 2 3 4 5 6 7 8 9 10
3. _____	1 2 3 4 5 6 7 8 9 10

Are there any requests for which you have begun to harbor doubts? If so, stop now and ask the Lord to renew your faith in Him and His provision.

Jesus had much to say about prayer. Carefully read the following two passages and note what Jesus taught.

"He also said to them: 'Suppose one of you has a friend and goes to him at midnight and says to him, "Friend, lend me three loaves of bread, because a friend of mind on a journey has come to me, and I don't have anything to offer him." Then he will answer from inside and say, "Don't bother me! The door is already locked, and my children and I have gone to bed. I can't get up to give you anything." I tell you, even though he won't get up and give him anything because he is his friend, yet because of his persistence, he will get up and give him as much as he needs. So I say to you, keep asking, and it will be given to you. Keep searching, and you will find. Keep knocking, and the door will be opened to you. For everyone who asks receives, and the one who searches finds, and to the one who knocks, the door will be opened.'"
Luke 11:5-10

"'There was a judge in one town who didn't fear God or respect man. And a widow in that town kept coming to him, saying, "Give me justice against my adversary." For a while he was unwilling, but later he said to himself, "Even though I don't fear God respect man, yet because this widow keeps pestering me, I will give her justice, so she doesn't wear me out by her persistent coming."' Then to Lord said, 'Listen to what the unjust judge says. Will not God grant justice to His elect who cry out to Him day and night? Will He delay to help them? I tell you that He will swiftly grant them justice.

Nevertheless, when the Son of Man comes, will he find that faith on earth?'" Luke 18:2-8

What lesson are we to learn from Jesus' parables in Luke 11 and 18?

In these parables Jesus used extreme examples to encourage people not to grow weary in praying. He claimed that even if these imperfect mortals would not help another out of the goodness of their hearts, they would eventually respond if pestered long enough! But of course, God is not a neglectful friend or an unjust judge. He is perfectly loving and just. He longs to respond to the requests of His people (see Jeremiah 33:3). The challenge is for God's people to persist in prayer until they receive an answer.

> **As we have seen from many of the stories in this study, praying for revival often requires a great deal of patience. Under each heading, list some of the temptations and distractions you see in your life and church which hinder believers from praying persistently for revival.**
> *Believers*   *Churches*

Too often, earnest people who pray for revival start well but lose their focus. They are like Peter when he got out of the boat and started walking on the water (see Matthew 8:23). He was steadily making his way to Jesus. But when he took his eyes off his Lord and noticed the waves lapping at his feet, he began to sink and fear for his life. Like Peter, those asking the Lord for revival begin well but soon focus on the problems rather than on the Savior, and their intercession for revival fades away.

What emotions do you associate with waiting for an answer from God?

How can these emotions encourage or distract your prayers?

Jesus told a story about 10 virgins who went to a wedding feast (see Matthew 25:1-13). Five failed to bring enough oil to keep their lamps lit until the bridegroom arrived to begin the banquet. When the bridegroom finally arrived, the five unprepared virgins were not admitted to the wedding feast. Again the point is made about staying power. Often we do not prepare ourselves for the possibility that our prayers' answers may be long in coming. How tragic for Christians who have prayed for years for God to bring revival to their church and then give up praying before God's answer comes.

Some people used to pray regularly for God to bring revival to their church. Time passed, and things only seemed to get worse. Eventually, they lost heart and gave up praying. Some simply found another church to attend and forgot about the burden God gave them to pray for the first congregation. By ceasing to pray, they chose no longer to participate in God's answer when He ultimately did His work.

Think about prayers you have offered for others in previous years. Record one request you have stopped praying because you did not see an answer.

Why did you stop praying?

What role will patience play in praying for revival?

Octavius Winslow suggests, "When a professing Christian can pray, and yet acknowledge that he has no nearness to the throne, no touching of the scepter, no fellowship with God,—calls him 'Father,' without the sense of adoption,—confesses sin in a general way, without any looking up to God through the cross,—has no consciousness of possessing the ear and the heart of God, the evidence is undoubted of a decline in the state of religion in the soul."[20]

Prayerless Christians are clear evidence of the urgent need for revival. If you have lost heart in praying, ask God to revive your soul so that you can once again intercede before God for those around you.

Encountering God in Prayer

Spend some prolonged time in prayer and ask the Lord to remind you of any prayer requests you have stopped praying before you saw His clear answer. Repent of your unfaithfulness in interceding for the needs of other believers and the salvation of the lost. As you speak to God today, commit yourself afresh to stay at your post in prayer until you witness God's clear answer.

Day 4 Praying Corporately

Praying in Korea

The members of a church in Korea once became so burdened for revival that they began to meet at five o'clock each morning to pray for it. They prayed for six months;

then revival came. Commending their commitment to pray, missionary Jonathan Goforth challenged North American Christians, "Do we really believe in God the Holy Spirit? Let us be honest. Not to the extent of getting up at five o'clock through six months of cold weather to seek Him!"[21] Christians of South Korea are renowned for their dedication to prayer. Is it any wonder that God has worked so powerfully in their nation in recent decades? Many church leaders from North America visit the massive churches in South Korea to gain insight into their phenomenal growth. Yet even though they have repeatedly been told it is due to prayer, most Westerners have not sought to duplicate the prayer efforts of their Korean brethren. It seems the temptation we often face is to duplicate program methodology and neglect intensive prayer.

Why do you think many churches adopt models for church growth techniques but place little emphasis on prayer?

Praying as One Body

Effective revival praying is both corporate and unified. Jesus declared, "Where two or three are gathered together in My name, I am among them" (Matthew 18:20). God has chosen to especially honor the prayers of unified Christians who cry out to Him. During the 1859 revival in Wales, someone observed that "a powerful spirit of prayer has laid hold of the churches."[22] Historians note that praying together for revival often brings about a spirit of unity in God's people.[23] During the Korean revival in 1907, Presbyterian and Methodist missionaries prayed together until prior feelings of antagonism or competition had disappeared. Once the church and mission leaders were unified in their desire for the Holy Spirit to bring revival, it came.[24] Tens of thousands of people were converted, although little had been done to evangelize them other than the unified prayers of God's people.

Think about your prayers with other believers.
Do you regularly meet with other believers to pray?   Yes   No

Identify any hindrances to unity for corporate prayer in your church or Bible-study group.

What answers have you seen to your corporate praying?

"It is written, 'My house will be a house of prayer,' but you have made it a den of thieves!"
Luke 19:46

Today's church sorely neglects praying together. Jesus boldly taught that His Father's house was to be a house of prayer (see Luke 19:46). Yet when His people pray during church gatherings, are our prayers characterized by impassioned cries to God for mercy and forgiveness? Too often, it seems that our public praying consists of a string of worn-out clichés that say little and merely ask for God to bless someone and to be with us. The body of Christ must realize that praying in clichés to God is as insulting as speaking in clichés to a spouse. All you communicate to the other party is that she does not matter enough for you to put any thought into the conversation. Certainly, our prayer lives should hold more value than any other conversation, because we are responding to God's invitation to learn what is on His heart.

During the great revival in Manchuria, many people were convicted and confessed their sins. However, others sought to appear spiritual before others even though their hearts were far from God. During one meeting a prominent church leader was praying a long, eloquent prayer. He seemed more concerned with impressing his listeners than communing with God. Jonathan Goforth went up to the man in exasperation and stopped him, exclaiming, "Please let's not have any of your ordinary kind of praying."[25]

What would Goforth think if he visited many of our churches today?

Much of the prayer that is modeled and commanded in the Bible is collective prayer. Jesus' model prayer uses the plural, "Our Father" (Matthew 6:9) and "Forgive us our debts" (Matthew 6:12). Jesus promised His disciples: "I assure you: Whatever you bind on earth is already bound in heaven, and whatever you loose on earth is already loosed in heaven. Again, I assure you: If two of you on earth agree about any matter that you pray for, it will be done for you by My Father in heaven. For where two or three are gathered together in My name, I am there among them" (Matthew 18:18-20). This Scripture is a profound promise! When God's people pray, God promises to answer in powerful ways. Believers can experience a unique sense of God's presence when they choose to pray with one heart and one mind (see Acts 4:31).

What are some reasons you think God particularly honors the prayers of those who pray together in unity?

How does praying with others in unity benefit our spiritual growth?

Many churches no longer offer any time in their schedule for their people to meet together to pray. The church calendar fills up with children's and youth events, choir practices, service times, Bible studies, outreach events, and men's and women's activities. There seems to be little time to squeeze in prayer. Certainly we are thankful for the opportunity to minister in these many ways but without prayer, we are

"When they had prayed, the place where they were assembled was shaken, and they were all filled with the Holy Spirit and began to speak God's message with boldness."
Acts 4:31

only relying on our own strength to do the ministry. No matter how lovingly we care for children, passionately we sing in worship, or carefully we reach out to the community—without a serious life of prayer for God's work in the church, at best, we will only draw a crowd of religious consumers and spectators.

In churches that still hold regular prayer times, only a small percentage of members attend. When many churches gather to pray, they spend only a small fraction of the time actually praying. There may be Bible teaching on prayer. Then someone reads a list of church members in the hospital, sick, unemployed, or having a birthday. Often only one or two church leaders are called on to pray, and then prayer meeting is dismissed for another week. Should we study God's Word? Absolutely. Should we pray for the "normal" needs of people. Yes. But when we overlook the need to confess sin, cry out for God's merciful visitation, and His reviving work in the church then we are missing out on some of the greatest prayer needs for the church today.

Surely this is not what God intended when He called the church a "house of prayer" (Isaiah 56:7; Matthew 21:13). Even the praying that takes place in worship services is often merely a brief string of clichés thrown together with little thought or preparation. Rarely is the entire congregation invited to participate in the prayer time. Today's church gives lip service to prayer but acts as if it can accomplish God's work without praying to Him about it. It is crucial that church leaders reverse this spiritually stifling trend. For God to be honored, congregations must be allowed to, encouraged to, and led to pray. Above all else, God's Word and prayer should set the church's agenda, not follow it.

For God to be honored, congregations must be allowed to, encouraged to, and led to pray.

Take a moment to reflect on your church's prayer life. Could your church truly be described as a "house of prayer"?

What does it indicate if we spend more time planning our church activities than praying for them?

How might your church make specific adjustments so that members have regular opportunities to pray together for their common concerns?

What can you personally do to help address the issue of praying for revival in your church?

The preceding paragraphs may have seemed harsh to you. Perhaps your church is truly a praying church, and you are witnessing an incredible movement of God's Spirit. Too many churches, however, are not. If you recognize the absence of prayer in your church, make sure you guard against developing a critical spirit. When God allows us to see a shortcoming in our church, it is not an invitation for us to criticize but to intercede. To gossip or complain about others merely adds our sin to theirs and thus compounds the problem. But when we immediately begin to pray with all our hearts for our church to become what God intends, God can use us as part of His solution to the problem we have observed.

Check ways you have responded to the needs and shortcomings of your church.

[ ] **Earnestly prayed for those involved**
[ ] **Complained**
[ ] **Gossiped**
[ ] **Given up**
[ ] **Encouraged those who were not doing all they should**
[ ] **Gathered others to pray for the problem**
[ ] **Sought to mind your own business**
[ ] **Other:**

You can assume that God placed you in your church for a reason. If it is not yet all it should be, meet with others and fervently, faithfully, righteously pray until God brings your church back into the relationship He wants to have with it.

Encountering God in Prayer

Reflect on your corporate prayer life. Do you regularly pray with others? Do you pray in unity? Are you a loner who does not pray with others? Take time to pray and to ask the Lord to show you how He wants you to begin regularly praying with others.

Day 5 Watchmen on the Walls

Praying for Others

We know a woman who is a prayer warrior; she spends many hours each week interceding for her church family. She prays for members by name. Often she feels impressed by the Holy Spirit that particular people have a special need, so she intensely intercedes for them. Her pastor and church leaders have often benefited from her intercession. One day this woman dropped by her pastor's office and explained that as she had prayed for him, she sensed he was facing a weighty decision. She did not ask what the decision was about; she had simply come to pray for him. As she prayed, everything she said related directly to his decision even though she knew none of the details. Over the next couple of weeks she occasionally stopped by to pray for her pastor. Eventually, she felt a sense of peace for her pastor, and she stopped interceding for that need. Although she did not know it, her pastor had received an invitation to lead another church, and he needed wisdom. Later, when he received a clear word not to accept the invitation, the woman sensed that her prayers were answered. She never interfered or asked for details; she was simply faithful to pray, and that was enough.

During church services this woman remained in the church's prayer room and interceded for those in the auditorium. Over the years she saw many answers to her prayers, and the church experienced numerous spiritual victories. Her congregation was fortunate to have a watchman standing at her post praying over them.

List some prayer needs of your church. Here are possible ideas to help you get started: repentance of corporate sin, greater concern for the poor in the city, greater heart for understanding God's Word, faith in difficult financial times, unity within the congregation, sharing God's passion for lost people, understanding God's plan for the future of the church, wisdom for Bible study leaders, and so forth.

Staying Spiritually Alert

Are you willing to adjust your lifestyle significantly enough to be the kind of prayer warrior God will use to change your family, your church, your city, your denomination, and your nation? God is looking for men and women of prayer who will intercede for those around them. God said through His prophet Isaiah,

> *"Jerusalem, I have appointed watchmen on your walls; they will never be silent, day or night. You, who remind the Lᴏʀᴅ, no rest for you! Do not give Him rest until He establishes and makes her Jerusalem the praise of the earth."* Isaiah 62:6-7

God looks at your heart to see whether you can be trusted with such an immense assignment.

The watchmen over a city held a critical post. Everyone within the city walls placed their lives in the hands of those who remained alert, watching for danger. Those who grew careless or slept at their post could cost men, women, and children their lives.

The position of spiritual watchman is not a voluntary one. It is an appointed position. God looks at your heart to see whether you can be trusted with such an immense assignment. He looks for those who will stay spiritually alert. He wants those on the walls for their family, church, and nation who will not grow weary or discouraged from watching but who will be found at their assigned post at all times. Being a spiritual watchman means you maintain your spiritual concentration so that you can detect the enemy's movements. You are alert to threats your church, family, or nation faces. You are quick to alert people when you see danger approaching. How blessed is the family that has a parent standing watch on the walls of the home. How fortunate is the church that has faithful prayer guardians praying on its behalf. How blessed is the nation with prayerful sentinels on the alert throughout the land.

If God has appointed you as a spiritual watchperson in your congregation, you can carry out this privileged assignment in several ways.

As you read the following list of ideas, check ways you feel led to serve as a spiritual sentry for your church.

[ ] **Talk to people of various ages in your church. Ask teenagers what they are facing. Talk with the seniors, middle-age couples, and young families. Listen without judging or necessarily offering advice. Ask God to give you a sensitive heart to what each person is facing. Observe what is happening during worship services and begin praying for anyone who seems to be under conviction or needs a fresh work of God.**

[ ] **Make yourself aware of what is happening in the community around your church. Are your teenagers facing new temptations? What new economic pressures are families facing?**

[ ] **Assure the church staff that you are lifting them up in prayer.**

[ ] **Regularly pray for specific members of your church, being sensitive to anything the Holy Spirit brings to your attention.**

[ ] **Be extremely careful to guard your heart and your motives. Like the woman mentioned earlier, you don't necessarily have to know all the details before you can pray. Allow the Holy Spirit to guide you. Be vigilant not to adopt a critical, judgmental, or gossipy attitude.**

The key is to ask the Lord for spiritual eyes to see what is happening around you and to be prepared to speak up when necessary.

Just as you can serve as a watchperson for your church, you can also be a watchperson for your family, business, community, or nation. The key is to ask the Lord for spiritual eyes to see what is happening around you and to be prepared to speak up when necessary.

Prophetic Messages

Sometimes God also appoints people to speak a word to His people on His behalf. The prophet Amos declared,

> *"Indeed, the Lord GOD does nothing without revealing His counsel to His servants the prophets."* Amos 3:7

God chooses to use people to share His desires and to reveal His activity. Prophets are unique in some ways, but they can also be extremely ordinary people. Amos said of himself, "I was not a prophet or the son of a prophet; rather, I was a herdsman, and I took care of sycamore figs. But the LORD took me from following the flock and said to me, 'Go, prophesy to My people Israel'" (Amos 7:14-15). Amos was an ordinary businessperson, but God chose to deliver a divine message through him. Similarly, Jeremiah was a young man and certainly did not see himself as a prophet when God called him (see Jeremiah 1:6). The 12 disciples were businesspeople when God called them and appointed them to proclaim His message. If God lets you see the spiritual danger people are facing, you will be held accountable for the way you alert those around you to the danger (see Ezekiel 33:1-11).

When Paul taught the Corinthian church about the spiritual gift of prophecy, he said, "Pursue love and desire spiritual gifts, and above all that you may prophesy. For the person who speaks in another language is not speaking to men but to God, since no one understands him; however, he speaks mysteries in the Spirit. But the person who prophesies speaks to people for edification, encouragement, and consolation" (1 Corinthians 14:1-3). Paul encouraged the early believers to seek ways God could use them to build up the body through this incredible gift. Too often when we think of a prophet for God, we imagine a cartoon-like character. The Bible teaches that a prophet is simply someone chosen by God to call His people to faithfully walk with Him and enjoy the sweet fellowship He offers us.

Why do you think there are not more spiritual watchmen today?

How might a watchman protect your family?

How might a watchman protect your church?

How might a watchman protect your community?

How might a watchman protect your nation?

What has God revealed to you that you need to share with others?

It is bold, confident praying, with the expectancy that God will hear and the assurance that He will answer.

People urgently need to hear from the Lord. God's judgment could be imminent. This age cries out for spiritual watchpersons and prophets to declare a word from the Lord. If your heart is devoted to God and you are prepared to stand watch for the spiritual welfare of those around you, don't be surprised if God gives you the words to speak that the people around you desperately need to hear.

Scripture is clear about the quality of praying that regularly sees results (see James 5:16). It is not halfhearted, lukewarm praying filled with qualifiers and escape clauses should God not accommodate the request. It is bold, confident praying, with the expectancy that God will hear and the assurance that He will answer. People who pray such prayers are not surprised when God answers them, for they fully expected as much. Christlike praying is not telling God what to do but seeking to understand what God has on His mind and then boldly asking Him to accomplish His heart's desire through whatever means He chooses. God delights in finding people who truly believe He will do what He promised (see Matthew 8:9-10).

Encountering God in Prayer

Could God be calling you to be a spiritual watchperson? Think of the various groups God has placed you in: family, church, denomination, community, and nation. Ask God to show you how He wants to use you as an intercessor on the walls of your family or church in the coming days. Ask God to open your spiritual eyes to see what is happening around you so you can more effectively pray for revival.

1. Adapted from Samuel I. Prime, *The Power of Prayer: Illustrated in the Wonderful Displays of Divine Grace at the Fulton Street and Other Meetings in New York and Elsewhere, in 1857 and 1858* (Pennsylvania: Banner of Truth Trust, 1991).
2. Ibid., 6.
3. Frank Grenville Beardsley, *A History of American Revivals* (Boston: American Tract Society, 1904), 216.
4. J. Edwin Orr, *The Event of the Century: The 1857–58 Awakening*, ed. Richard Owen Roberts (Wheaton, IL: International Awakening Press, 1989), 338.
5. Colin and Mary Peckham, *Sounds from Heaven: The Revival on the Isle of Lewis, Scotland, 1949–1952* (Ross-shire, Scotland: Christian Focus Publications, 2004), 113.
6. Duncan Campbell, *The Price and Power of Revival* (Fort Washington, PA: Christian Literature Crusade, n.d.), 67.
7. Arthur Wallis, *In the Day of Your Power: A Picture of Revival from Scripture and History* (Columbia, MO: City Hill Publishing, 1990), 211.
8. E. M. Bounds, *Power Through Prayer : Preacher and Prayer* (Grand Rapids: Zondervan Publishing House, 1968), 27.
9. Brian Edwards, *Revival! A People Saturated with God* (Durham, England: Evangelical Press, 1995), 84.
10. Wallis, *In the Day of Your Power,* 211.
11. Campbell, *The Price and Power of Revival,* 18.
12. James Alexander Stewart, *William Chambers Burns, Robert Murray McCheyne* (Alexandria, LA: Lamplighter Publications, n.d.), 21.
13. Ibid., 44.
14. Richard Owen Roberts, ed., *Scotland Saw His Glory* (Wheaton, IL: International Awakening Press, 1995), 128.
15. D. Macfarlan, *The Revivals of the Eighteenth Century, Particularly at Cambuslang* (Wheaton, IL: Richard Owen Roberts Publishers, 1980), 35.
16. Roberts, ed., *Scotland Saw His Glory,* 132.
17. Ibid., 137.
18. Wallis, *In the Day of Your Power,* 188.
19. Basil Miller, *George Müller: The Man of Faith* (Grand Rapids: Zondervan Publishing House, 1941), 145–46.
20. Octavius Winslow, *Personal Declension and Revival of Religion in the Soul* (Pennsylvania: The Banner of Truth Trust, 1978), 18.
21. Jonathan Goforth, *When the Spirit's Fire Swept Korea* (Grand Rapids: Zondervan Publishing House, 1958), 17.
22. Thomas Phillips, *The Welsh Revival: Its Origin and Development* (Pennsylvania: The Banner of Truth Trust, 1989), 21.
23. Ibid., 49.
24. Goforth, *When the Spirit's Fire Swept Korea,* 8.
25. Jonathan Goforth, *By My Spirit* (Grand Rapids: Zondervan Publishing House, 1942), 34.

Small-Group Discussion Guide

⚜ † ⚜

Open in prayer.

Ahead of time, ask someone to be prepared to pray. Invite prayer requests and ask the group for prayer requests that pertain to personal and corporate revival. Listen for how God is presently working in their lives through the study so that the group will know how to pray for them. Once people have had an opportunity to share, call on the person appointed to pray.

View Session 5 of the Teaching DVD

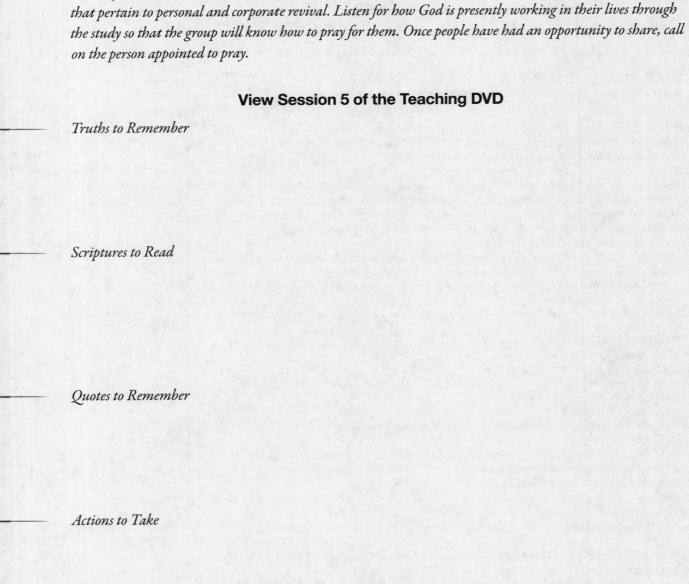

Truths to Remember

Scriptures to Read

Quotes to Remember

Actions to Take

If you missed this session, go to *www.lifeway.com/freshencounter* to download this and any other session of *Fresh Encounter.*

Discussion Guide

Ask group members to share what God taught them about praying for revival this week.

Have you begun to pray differently as a result of what you have learned?

Call on volunteers to share their reactions to the DVD.

What does the story of Jeremiah Lanphier (p. 121) encourage you to do concerning prayer for revival?

Discuss actions that your group or church could take to encourage believers to consistently pray for revival and spiritual awakening.

Mark 11:23-24 is an incredible invitation to prayer by Jesus. Have someone in the group read these verses.

What is the proper understanding of how we can receive anything for which we ask?

What role does the phrase "in My name" have in our prayers to God?

God uses prayer to shape our passions to mirror His own.

How have you seen your passions and priorities change through prayer?

Why do people struggle to pray when everyone is capable of doing it?

The Blackabys point out that prayer is a relationship rather than an experience.

How does this truth aid us in praying more consistently and with greater faith?

Ask group members to discuss the role of a watchman on the walls.

Which is hardest—to pray in faith, righteously, or persistently?

How do you sense God wants to help you improve your prayer life so you can fulfill such a spiritual role?

God desires that we pray with passion concerning the things for which He is passionate.

If given a test, how would you rate items like "desperation for revival" and "desire for all people to understand the gospel" in your prayer life?

How should you change the way you pray in order to grow increasingly closer to God and align yourself with His will?

Spend the remainder of the time praying. Seek to incorporate into your prayers lessons learned this week.

Close in prayer.

UNIT 6: PEOPLE GOD USES IN REVIVAL

Scripture-Memory Verse

"When they had prayed, the place where they were assembled was shaken, and they were all filled with the Holy Spirit and began to speak God's message with boldness."

ACTS 4:31

Unit Overview

DAY 1: GOD USES ORDINARY PEOPLE

DAY 2: GOD USES PASSIONATE PEOPLE

DAY 3: GOD USES PRAYERFUL AND ACTIVE PEOPLE

DAY 4: GOD USES SACRIFICIAL PEOPLE

DAY 5: GOD USES PEOPLE WHO GIVE HIM THE GLORY

Cleansing by Washing with Water Through the Word

"Christ loved the church and gave Himself for her, to make her holy, cleansing her in the washing of water by the word. He did this to present the church to Himself in splendor, without spot or wrinkle or any such thing, but holy and blameless." Ephesians 5:25-27

Wash Out

Are there actions, behaviors, habits, or sins that need to be cleansed from your life, family, or church? Confess them (agree with God about the wrongdoing), turn away from them, and turn to God.

Soak In

Are there good things that need to be absorbed into your life and relationships? Pray about those and seek to become all God wants you to be.

- → **Exodus 3:9-12**
- → **Isaiah 6:8**
- → **Isaiah 52:7**
- → **Jeremiah 1:5**
- → **Mark 1:16-20**
- → **2 Timothy 1:9**
- → **2 Timothy 2:15**

Keep the verses above in mind as you work through the Bible studies this week. Use the space below to keep a list of the specific lessons you learn from your studies and how God is applying these lessons to your life.

In a Coal Miner's Life

Evan Roberts labored as a coal miner from the age of 12. The work was arduous, but he always carried his Bible with him to read during breaks. For 11 years this young man earnestly prayed that God would send revival to his native land of Wales. In 1904, when he was 26, Roberts sensed God leading him to enroll at the preparatory school in Newcastle Emlyn. Later that fall Roberts joined a team of young people accompanying the evangelist Seth Joshua while he conducted a meeting in Blaenanerch. Roberts was deeply moved by Joshua's sermon but even more impacted by his closing prayer. Joshua prayed, "Bend us, O Lord." Roberts heard the Spirit of God tell him, "This is what you need." Roberts prayed, "Bend me, O Lord."[1] Roberts was an uneducated, untrained coal miner; but he sensed God asking him to completely surrender his life to His hands.

Roberts returned to his home church in Loughor and asked his pastor if he could address the people gathered at the evening service. The pastor invited anyone who wished to hear Roberts to remain behind after the regular service. With that group of 17 people, Roberts shared what God had been saying to him about revival. The Spirit of God descended on that humble gathering, and revival burst forth. Roberts's motto became "Bend the church and save the world."

Word soon spread across the country that revival had come. Services were conducted all across the land and often lasted until late into the night. Tens of thousands of people were gloriously converted. It was said that the coal mines were so transformed that the pit ponies that hauled coal out of the mines were temporarily immobilized because they did not understand the commands that were now devoid of profanity! By the end of December, only two months after the revival began, 70,000 people had been converted and added to the churches. After six months the number of converts reached 100,000. The revival of the church spread around the world, resulting in the conversion of thousands of lost people. One simple laborer sought to be pliable in God's hands, and the world felt the impact.

⚜ † ⚜

God Uses Ordinary People

Flee or Preach?

IN SURVEYS ABOUT WHAT PEOPLE FEAR THE MOST, PUBLIC SPEAKING NEARLY ALWAYS RANKS FIRST. People often claim they are more terrified of speaking in public than they are of death! Such was the case for a young minister at the Kirk of Shotts in Scotland on June 21, 1630. People from all over the region had gathered for a massive communion service. When the appointed preacher became ill and was unable to preach, the remaining ministers decided John Livingston should take his place. It was an unexpected occurrence.

Livingston, a young pastor, had never delivered such an important sermon before. Many of the clergy present had far more experience than he did. As throngs of people gathered for the service, Livingston panicked and contemplated fleeing the scene rather than embarrassing himself. He later confessed, "Considering my unworthiness and weakness, and the multitude and expectation of the people, … I was consulting with myself to have stolen away somewhere and declined that day's preaching."[2] Yet even as he prepared to escape, the Holy Spirit assured him he was God's appointed messenger for that day and would enable him to speak. Livingston preached from Ezekiel 36:25-26, and five hundred people were converted.[3] The reluctant minister discovered that when it comes to delivering a message from God, it doesn't matter how important you are but how anointed.

What Can I Do?

What can you do to bring revival to your church? Around the world people recognize that their church desperately needs a fresh moving of the Holy Spirit, but they have no idea how to bring it about. During our study this week, we will identify eight characteristics you need for God to use you as a catalyst for revival.

1. People Who Are Ordinary

If there is anything the Bible and church history teach, it is that God is willing to use the most ordinary people to initiate renewal. He is not limited by worldly concerns such as the size of a congregation, the eloquence of a speaker, or the educational level of His servant.

God often chooses to accomplish His sovereign purposes by using ordinary people.

The life-giving God can restore any person or any church to spiritual vitality. Revival is a divine work. So, we often ask, "What can one person, one pastor, or one small group of people do to lift a church out of its lethargy?" Yet, God often chooses to accomplish His sovereign purposes by using ordinary people. As God was seeking people who would accomplish His work, He said through the prophet Ezekiel, "I searched for a man among them who would repair the wall and stand in the gap before Me on behalf of the land so that I might not destroy it, but I found no one. So

I have poured out My indignation on them and consumed them with the fire of My fury. I have brought their actions down on their own heads" (Ezekiel 22:30-31).

From the previous passage, list the actions God was looking for someone to do.

Now list the consequences if God did not find someone to do these things.

Does God need to use people to accomplish His work? No. He is able to accomplish any work on His own. Plus, God has a myriad of powerful angels ready and eager to do His bidding. Nonetheless, God chooses to do His mighty work through weak, ordinary human instruments. If God always used His magnificent angels or the most impressive people to achieve His purposes, many people would inevitably value the agents and rely on them rather than God. But when He uses ordinary people as His agents, only God can receive the recognition for the work accomplished.

List several of your greatest spiritual concerns about:

Family:

Church:

Nation:

Write down ways God might want to use you to make a difference in those situations.

Whom Does God Use?

Much has been written about the type of person through whom God works to accomplish His divine purposes. One thing is certain: God's standard is different from the world's.

Read 1 Samuel 16:7. When the Lord sent Samuel to select a king from among Jesse's sons, what quality did He value more than any other?

[ ] **Strength**
[ ] **Wisdom**
[ ] **Heart**
[ ] **Wealth**

"The Lord said to Samuel, 'Do not look at his appearance or his stature, because I have rejected him. Man does not see what the Lord sees, for man sees what is visible, but the Lord sees the heart.' "
1 Samuel 16:7

The world assumes that people of spiritual influence must be charismatic leaders, inspiring communicators, and effective administrators. Although these attributes may be helpful, they can also be liabilities. Brian Edwards observed, "We have our leaders today, but rarely do they have the mark of God's Spirit upon them. They have become leaders by denominational progression or by their force of character, or by their organizing ability and their capacity for hard work."[4] Biblically and historically, one of the most surprising characteristics of those used mightily by God is how ordinary they were.

One relentless critique leveled at revival movements has been the imperfection of its leaders. God powerfully used Evan Roberts to bring spiritual awakening to Wales, but within six months he was worn-out and withdrew from public life. Charles Finney was criticized for his adoption of seemingly worldly methods in his revival meetings. D. L. Moody was so uneducated that some people attended his meetings merely to mock his poor grammar. Yet as Thomas Phillips notes, "The weakness of the instrument is no argument against the reality of the work."[5] Revival leaders' evident frailties and mistakes merely highlight the fact that these people were engaged in a work far greater than themselves.

Brian Edwards has noted that historical accounts rarely gave a detailed physical description of revival leaders.[6] Perhaps their appearance, style of dress, or other external features were deemed irrelevant to the effectiveness of their ministry. J. Edwin Orr observed that the only distinguishing mark of James McGready, a powerful catalyst for revival on the American frontier in the early 1800s, was that he was one of the ugliest men west of the Alleghenies! George Whitefield was nicknamed "Dr. Squintum" because of the way he peered at people. Indeed, like Moses and Gideon, some of the men and women who became key instruments for revival almost passed up their divine assignments because they assumed they were too ordinary for God to use.

List two or three reasons or obstacles that would prevent God from using you to address revival and spiritual awakening in your family, church, and community.

Read Isaiah 40:1–41:10. Now take a fresh look at your reasons. Describe the scope of God's power in your own words.

Looking at Isaiah 41:8-10, how do you believe God can use you?

Why do you think God would prefer to use an ordinary person rather than an unusually talented person to accomplish His work?

God's Hand

It might sound humble to say, "I am too ordinary or untalented for God to use me to do anything important." But when we claim God cannot use us to change our church or family or world, we are saying more about our belief in God than we are about our own ability. In essence, we are claiming that even all-powerful God is not mighty enough to use an instrument as ordinary as us!

William Chambers Burns was a young missionary appointee who agreed to preach temporarily in his native Scotland while waiting to sail to China. Burns is described this way: "Young, inexperienced, measured and slow of speech, gifted with no peculiar charm of poetry or sentiment or natural eloquence or winning sweetness."[7] That does not sound like the kind of person to be entrusted with even the most modest church assignment. Yet the same commentator also observed, "He bore so manifestly the visible seals of a divine commission, and carried about him withal such an awe of the divine presence and majesty, as to disarm criticism and constrain even careless hearts to receive him as the messenger of God."[8] God used Burns as His instrument to bring revival to the church in which he was the interim pastor while the church's beloved minister, Robert Murray McCheyne, was traveling abroad. Does God use skilled and famous people for His work? Certainly. But history is replete with examples when God chose an ordinary man or woman to accomplish His heavenly purposes.

Consider whether God wants to do far more through your life than you have yet been willing to believe. What are some things you have struggled to believe God could do through you?

Take some time to pray over each one to learn whether God is inviting you to trust Him for a miracle.

Encountering God in Prayer and Action

Take time in prayer to thank God that He does not merely use spiritual superstars to get His work done. Instead, He specializes in using ordinary people. Ask God to forgive you if you have underestimated your potential as His servant. Carefully take inventory of your thoughts regarding God's power to use you. If necessary, repent of thinking too lowly of God. Today, surrender your life afresh to His will and take the next step of action He leads you to take.

Day 2 God Uses Passionate People

Revival Through Video

Henry once received an unusual phone call late one Sunday evening from a church in Texas. The congregation had been going through a tumultuous time of infighting. Members were angry at one another, and business meetings routinely degenerated into shouting matches. During this time a small group of members had been meeting on Sunday evenings before the evening service to study *Experiencing God*. This group was burdened over the spiritual condition of the church but did not know what to do. One week the *Experiencing God* video explored the subject of churches functioning as God intended. That evening a special business meeting was called to deliberate a contentious issue. Amid the angry shouts and accusations someone suggested that they pause and watch the video in the business session. As they listened to the biblical teaching, the Holy Spirit descended on the congregation. People began to weep as they realized how far they had departed from God's standard. Members left their seats and began to reconcile with one another. Men and women stood to publicly confess their sins. Revival had come! The person who called Henry excitedly told him that the meeting was continuing late into the evening as people reconciled with God and with one another.

God uses ordinary people for His kingdom work but not just any ordinary people. God delights to work through people who are passionate about Him and His Word.

How would you describe your relationship with God?

[ ] **Nonexistent**
[ ] **Apathetic**
[ ] **Average**
[ ] **Passionate**

2. People with a Passion for God

Too many churches try to schedule a revival meeting on the church calendar as if it were the same type of event as a potluck dinner. It cannot be scheduled. Revival comes when people grow desperate for it. It happens when God's people become sickened with their worldliness and foolish rebellion against their Creator and return to Him with all of their heart, mind, soul, and strength. For revival to occur today, God's people must seek Him with an entirely new level of urgency.

Seeking revival is seeking the relationship with God, not the benefits of the relationship.

Seeking revival is seeking the relationship with God, not the benefits of the relationship. Duncan Campbell once asked, "How many today are really prepared to face the stark fact that we have been out maneuvered by the strategy of hell, because we tried to meet the enemy on human levels by human strategy? In this we may have succeeded in making people church-conscious, mission-conscious, or even crusade conscious, without making them God-conscious."[9] It was said of Robert Murray McCheyne that "he sought after God as fervently and assiduously as miners seek after gold."[10] As a result, McCheyne's church experienced showers of revival. It does not always take a multitude to launch a revival movement, but there must be a catalyst. If even a handful of people urgently and desperately seek God, it does not take long for the entire church to feel the impact. The key is not to strive for revival but to seek God wholeheartedly.

Could you say with all honesty and sincerity that you are wholly consumed with knowing and experiencing God? How do your actions manifest evidence of a passion for God?

Read the consuming quest of the apostle Paul's life from Philippians:

"Everything that was a gain to me, I have considered to be a loss because of Christ. More than that, I also consider everything to be a loss in view of the surpassing value of knowing Christ Jesus my Lord. Because of Him I have suffered the loss of all things and consider them filth, so that I may gain Christ and be found in Him, not having a righteousness of my own from the law, but one that is through faith in Christ—the righteousness from God based on faith. My goal is to know Him and the power of His resurrection and the fellowship of His sufferings, being conformed to His death." Philippians 3:7-10

What did Paul want to gain?

Review your daily schedule. What will you gain from the activities that consume most of your time and energy?

What should you count as rubbish in order to become more passionate about Christ?

It is possible to become so distracted by the problems in your church, family, or nation that you neglect to focus on God. In the verses above, underline everything Paul was willing to do to know Christ. Consider what your own focus is. Are you like Paul, or are distractions and concerns keeping you from knowing Christ better?

The Priority of Christ

At the beginning of this week, we read about Evan Roberts and the Great Awakening in Wales. The revival began when Roberts returned to his home church in Loughor and spoke to 17 people after the evening service. Roberts shared four basic requirements he believed God was looking for in His people:

1. You must put away any unconfessed sin.
2. You must put away any doubtful habit.
3. You must promptly obey the Holy Spirit.
4. You must publicly confess Christ.[11]

Roberts urged his small audience to agree to keep these obligations to God. It was an inauspicious beginning to an enormous work of God. The young Welshman exhorted his fellow church members to share his passion for God. By following these four simple commitments, those people witnessed a massive revival in their midst that shook their nation and beyond.

God is looking for people who will embrace what is on His heart and mind (see 1 Samuel 2:35). If you can go for weeks and not feel burdened for God to bring revival to your life, your church, or your nation, cry out to God to place His loving heart over yours. God is not willing for anyone to perish (see 2 Peter 3:9). Ask God to give you His burden for revival. Then your heart will break to know that millions eternally perish each year. Then your heart will grieve with God's that so many people are far from Him. Then, you will have the weeping heart of Jesus for those who are held in bondage to their sin (see Luke 19:41-42). If you already have such a concern, keep that passion constantly before you until you see God answer your prayers.

Passion should result in action. Think about your passion to see revival in the church and spiritual awakening in your community. What actions are you taking in your church to be used by God in revival?

What actions are you taking among your unbelieving friends to lead to understand the gospel and follow Christ?

3. People Committed to God's Word

A third characteristic of those God uses as catalysts for revival is that they are committed to believe and obey what God says in His Word. God keeps His promises. He is absolutely faithful to His Word. Too many Christians neglect to claim God's promises for their own lives and for their church, so they never see them fulfilled. Arthur Wallis stated about claiming God's promises in faith, "This is a spiritual lever that never fails to move the hand that moves the world."[12] Time and time again when people have investigated the antecedents of a great moving of God, they have

"I will raise up a faithful priest for Myself. He will do whatever is in My heart and mind. I will establish a lasting dynasty for him, and he will walk before My anointed one for all time"
1 Samuel 2:35

"The Lord does not delay His promise, as some understand delay, but is patient with you, not wanting any to perish, but all to come to repentance."
2 Peter 3:9

invariably traced the divine work back to some person or group who thoroughly believed God would keep His promises.

List three of God's promises in Scripture that you are presently believing and watching for Him to carry out in your life and in the lives of those around you. Write the Scripture verse beside the promise.

If you cannot think of any promises you are actively claiming in your life, how do you think that is affecting your experience of God's working in your life?

If you were unable to think of any promises, consider reading the following verses and write how you hope they will be fulfilled in your life.

> **Matthew 28:20:**

> **Romans 6:6-7:**

> **Romans 8:15-17:**

> **Ephesians 2:6-10:**

God revives people who obey His Word and trust Him to keep His promises. Whether it is a church member like Evan Roberts who urged fellow Christians to obey God's Word or a pastor like Jonathan Edwards who faithfully taught and preached God's Word every week, Scripture is always the foundation for revival. It was said that in Scotland at the beginning of the 1800s, "the people were very generally as ignorant of the Scriptures and Scripture truth as the inhabitants of Hindostan [India]."[13] Yet William McCulloch, the minister at Cambuslang, faithfully taught the Scriptures to his people. Although he did not realize it at first, the steady diet of biblical teaching was laying a solid foundation for the great revival that would eventually come.

Though God has used traumatic events, natural disasters, and personal testimonies to spark revival, the greatest movements of God throughout church history have always come on the foundation of Scripture and biblical preaching. While Jonathan Edwards' famous sermon "Sinners in the Hands of an Angry God" is best known for its stunning effect on its listeners, Edwards was helping his people clearly understand the truth of the Scriptures as found in Deuteronomy 32:35. Less known is that another season of revival came under Edwards's tenure in 1740 after he preached a series of sermons on the love of Christ from 1 Corinthians 13.[14] It was not so much dramatic preaching that impacted people as it was the careful exposition and application of God's Word that lifted them out of their spiritual lethargy.

How many days each week do you intentionally study the Bible?

In addition to personal Bible study, what are some practical ways you could expose yourself to solid, frequent Bible teaching?

Choose a Bible passage you have recently read and write down the impact it could have on a friend with whom you can share it.

When even a few Christians are impacted by God's Word and are inspired to strive for holiness, the rest of the church will feel the impact.

Obviously, a pastor is in a strategic position to bring scriptural truth to God's people. But laypersons can also help build a biblical foundation for revival in their church. We have seen God powerfully use Bible teachers to spiritually refresh adults in their church. Home Bible studies throughout the week have played key roles in revivals. Teenagers who have encountered God under the teaching of youth leaders have eventually brought renewal to their entire church. When even a few Christians are impacted by God's Word and are inspired to strive for holiness, the rest of the church will feel the impact. We have heard how small groups studying *Experiencing God* have been catalysts to bring revival to churches and Christian organizations around the world. Perhaps God will use your group in this study to do the same!

Simply being an ordinary person is not enough to be used mightily by God. You must also have a passion for Him and a total commitment to believe and to obey His Word. When God finds someone like that, there is no limit to what He can do.

Without obedience to God's Word, your study is incomplete. Are there lessons you have learned from God's Word but have not yet obeyed? If so, this sin could be the hindrance to revival in your church. A great temptation faced by the church is to increase its knowledge of the Bible but not its practice of the biblical teachings learned. Critical to revival's coming is for God's people to both study and practice the truth in His Word.

Encountering God in Prayer and Action

Take time today to enjoy being in God's presence through prayer. Focus on Him. Listen to Him. Read great promises of God from the Bible and meditate on them. Ask God how He wants to make those promises a reality in your life. Make a note of what He says so that you can recognize His activity in your life. Be sure to obey anything the Lord shows you through His Word.

Day 3 God Uses Prayerful and Active People

Seeking Revival from Bed

In 1872 D. L. Moody sailed for Great Britain. At that time Moody was relatively unknown outside the United States, and he was unsure what the Lord would have for him when he arrived. A congregational minister invited him to preach at Arundel Square near the Pentonville Prison in a lower-class neighborhood in England. The people's response to Moody's preaching during the Sunday-morning service was less than enthusiastic, and Moody wondered whether he had made a mistake in agreeing to come. However, he was unaware that a woman hurried home after the service to report the morning's events to her bedridden younger sister, Marianne Adlard.

When she told Marianne that Moody had preached at their church that morning, Marianne excitedly pulled out from under her pillow a newspaper report about Moody's work in Chicago. "I know what that means! God has heard my prayers!" Marianne exclaimed.[15] Ever since she had read about Moody in the newspaper, she had pleaded with God to send him to revive her church. As that evening's service began, there was unusual excitement in the atmosphere. At the close of Moody's sermon, he asked anyone who wanted to accept Christ to stand so that he could pray for them. So many people rose to their feet that Moody assumed they had misunderstood what he said. He had them sit back down, and he carefully explained that only those wanting to accept Christ as their Savior should adjourn to another room, where others could counsel them. That room filled up with people seeking God. Moody preached during the week to that congregation, and more than four hundred people were added to the church. When later asked what brought the spiritual breakthrough, Moody believed it was the faithful prayers of the invalid young woman who claimed God's promises for her beloved congregation.

4. People Committed to Prayer

We have seen that God uses ordinary people who are passionate about God and His Word to bring revival. But an essential component of every revival is prayer. Duncan Campbell said, "The early Church put power before influence. ... Power, not influence, was the watchword of the early Church."[16] Not everyone is equipped to preach stirring revival sermons to their congregation, nor is everyone in a position of leadership to make decisions for their church. But these are not the most important actions you can take to encourage revival. Talking with God about your situation is the most significant thing you can do. Along with interceding individually, pray with others. Don't use your prayer meetings to discuss the church's programs or the pastor's shortcomings. Simply intercede for your church with all your heart. Allow God to lay His broken heart for your church over your heart so that you begin to see your church's problems from His eternal perspective. Regularly and reverently praying

Talking with God about your situation is the most significant thing you can do.

Allow God to lay His broken heart for your church over your heart so you begin to see your church's problems from God's eternal perspective.

with a growing number of people for your church or denomination or nation will make a difference.

God looks for spiritual advocates on behalf of people and their sins. In Ezekiel 22:30-31 God said, " 'I searched for a man among them who would repair the wall and stand in the gap before Me on behalf of the land so that I might not destroy it, but I found no one. So I have poured out My indignation on them and consumed them with the fire of My fury. I have brought their actions down on their own heads.' This is the declaration of the Lord God." Obviously, our prayers on behalf of His people matter.

Earlier in Israel's history Moses petitioned the Lord on the people's behalf when God was prepared to annihilate them:

"LORD, why does Your anger burn against Your people You brought out of the land of Egypt with great power and a strong hand? Why should the Egyptians say, "He brought them out with an evil intent to kill them in the mountains and wipe them off the face of the earth"? Turn from Your great anger and change Your mind about this disaster planned for Your people. Remember that You swore to Your servants Abraham, Isaac, and Israel by Yourself and declared to them, "I will make your offspring as numerous as the stars of the sky and will give your offspring all this land that I have promised, and they will inherit it forever."' So the LORD changed His mind about the disaster He said He would bring on His people." Exodus 32:11-14

The next day Moses petitioned God to forgive the sin of His people: "Oh, this people has committed a great sin; they have made for themselves a god of gold. Now if You would only forgive their sin. But if not, please erase me from the book You have written" (Exodus 32:31-32). Moses was willing to take on the penalty and suffering of the people; his was not just casual, safe praying! Although Moses' heartfelt intercession could not remove the guilt of the people's sin, it spared the people from immediate judgment.

We cannot fully understand why God chooses to involve us in the process of others' salvation and revival. But clearly, He does so. Of course, God does not depend on human instruments to accomplish His work, so He does not need to have people praying in order for Him to act. However, those who accept His invitation to intercede on behalf of their family or their church enter new dimensions of communion with God as their hearts become like His.

Moses was willing to take on the penalty and suffering of the people; his was not just casual, safe praying!

Review the passage about Moses' intercession. What was God's response to Moses' passionate prayer?

Has there ever been a time when you prayed to God with that level of fervency? If so, what was the cause? If not, why not?

List people for whom you are presently interceding with God. Beside each name, state what you are asking God to do in their lives.

If you are not praying for revival, you cannot expect God to use your life as an instrument for revival.

5. People Committed to Working with Others

To be a catalyst for revival one must be willing and able to work with others. One reason humble, continuous prayer is so crucial is the safeguarding effect it has on the person praying. The fact is, those who are the most outspoken about the need for repentance and revival are not always speaking from God's heart. Some people feel called to be prophets; they fearlessly denounce people's sins and adamantly point out the shortcomings of their church. Yet in Scripture the prophet's arrival meant God was using His last resort before He sent judgment. By the time a prophet arrived on the scene, the people were usually so calloused that they murdered God's messenger, and judgment came. Though sin is sin and must be denounced, some people are loners who feel their role is to be a voice crying in the wilderness. Brian Edwards said, "Rarely will revival come as a result of one man's praying."[17] "Lone Ranger" Christians rarely motivate others toward revival. Those who remain inside the church loving and praying with others, rather than those who stand outside the church shouting condemnation, bring the church back into a loving relationship with God.

On the continuum below, rank how involved you are in working with others to advance God's kingdom and revival.

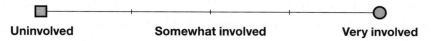

Uninvolved   Somewhat involved   Very involved

List the people with whom you are actively working to seek God's revival in the church. Examples could be your pastor, a Bible-study teacher, other staff members, and friends. List them by name and take a few moments to pray for God's power in their lives.

Those seeking revival do not compromise the truth of the Scriptures. Neither do they seek revival by shouting accusations from a distance. We must be like Jesus, who left heaven and walked among sinful people in order to bring them salvation. Without compromising truth, He drew sinners to Himself and set many free from their sins.

How do you think people in your church view you? Circle all that apply.

Supportive	Burdened for unbelievers
Positive attitude	Supportive of church leaders
Critical spirit	Sensitive to the Holy Spirit
Divisive	Gives up easily
Judgmental	Trustworthy
Prayerful	Has integrity

List at least five things you are presently doing with other believers to further God's purposes for revival and spiritual awakening.

1.

2.

3.

4.

5.

Working with Others

The story of Nehemiah in the Old Testament provides a biblical example of how God used a man to work alongside others to seek the revival of the people of God. When Nehemiah saw the pitiful condition of God's people, he took action and drew them together. Nehemiah never condoned the sinful practices or conditions he found. In fact, he spent much of his time confronting the sinfulness of God's people. He found ways to take God's people from where they were to where God wanted them to be. With the help of Ezra the priest and the other spiritual leaders of Israel, a host of God's people were revived and served the Lord.

He found ways to take God's people from where they were to where God wanted them to be.

Jeremiah Lanphier knew how to work with others. He could have stood outside the New York Stock Exchange condemning the vice and greed that were widespread in his day. He could have stormed into the churches and denounced the materialism that had overtaken them. Instead, he called people of all denominations to pray, and he helped them see that God had something better for them than the mere pursuit of wealth. As a result, when the stock market crashed in 1857, God's people were already meeting regularly to pray for the nation. The church was poised to turn their nation back to God in revival.

If you find yourself constantly battling with others and standing out as the lone critic of your church and its leaders, return to God and ask Him to examine your heart. Critics may highlight weaknesses, but they are seldom used as instruments of revival.

Reflect on your relationships.
Are you living as an ambassador for Christ? Yes No
Are you a catalyst who brings other people together? Yes No
Are you a peacemaker? Yes No
Is God using you to take people into a deeper walk with Him? Yes No
Is God using your life to bring sinners to salvation? Yes No
Do others want to pray because you pray? Yes No
Do others want to be more faithful because they observe your faithfulness? Yes No

Encountering God in Prayer and Action

Look back at the list of people for whom you are interceding (p. 159). Take the remainder of this time to fervently cry out to God on their behalf.

Day 4 God Uses Sacrificial People

Paying the Price for Revival in China

Jonathan Goforth was a missionary to China during the early 20th century. For 13 years he faithfully ministered to people, but he began to sense that much of what he was doing was merely religious activity devoid of spiritual power. He wrote, "I began to experience a growing dissatisfaction with the results of my work. In the early pioneer years I had buoyed myself with the assurance that a seed-time must always precede a harvest, and had, therefore, been content to persist in the apparently futile struggle. But now thirteen years had passed, and the harvest seemed, if anything, farther away than ever. I felt sure that there was something larger ahead of me, if I only had the vision to see what it was, and the faith to grasp it."[18]

Goforth came to realize that a broken relationship between a fellow missionary was preventing him from experiencing God's power in his life. Despite considering himself innocent and his colleague the offender, Goforth sensed that he would not experience God's power until he reconciled with his fellow missionary. When Goforth apologized to the man, God's power was poured out on Goforth in his subsequent ministry. Everywhere Goforth went afterward, the Holy Spirit powerfully worked through him to revive God's people and to bring numerous others to belief in Christ. Goforth had been willing to pray more, to read his Bible more, and to work harder; but humbling himself before someone he felt had harmed him was the most difficult thing he could have done. Yet that was the very thing standing between him and the presence of God's power in his life and ministry.

6. People Willing to Pay the Price

God doesn't work powerfully through revival in response to a whimsical, halfhearted effort. People God has used as an impetus for revival have been willing to pay a greater price than their contemporaries. Oswald Sanders challenged, "The spirit of the welfare state does not produce leaders. If a Christian is not willing to rise early and work late, to expend greater effort in diligent study and faithful work, that person will not change a generation. Fatigue is the price of leadership. Mediocrity is the result of never getting tired."[19]

"Fatigue is the price of leadership. Mediocrity is the result of never getting tired."

—Oswald Sanders

Reflect on Oswald Sanders's statement. Do you agree? Why or why not?

When Seth Joshua prayed and asked God to bend the church, Evan Roberts prayed, "Bend me!"[20] Roberts understood that the key to revival was not for God to change everyone else but for God to have complete access to his life. Roberts could have fixated on the shortcomings of others. Instead, he zeroed in on the one person he had control over: himself. To be a driving force for revival, Roberts would have to be a pliable instrument in God's hands. Revival is costly. That is why so few people are involved in it. Once revival has come and the crowds are excitedly gathering each evening, many people are willing to participate and preach. But the work of spiritual cultivation for revival is laborious and demanding, and many lose heart before the sought-after revival comes. The saintly Robert Murray McCheyne said, "There is a great want about all Christians who have not suffered."[21] Some ministers are appalled at George Whitefield's quip that he'd rather "burn out than rust out." Though seminaries emphasize balance and health for church ministers, but young ministers must also be taught what price must be paid for God to work mightily in revival.

Revival is costly. That is why so few people are involved in it.

In past times, such as in George Whitefield's era, God powerfully used many people in revival, and there were regular periods of renewal and awakening. There have been seasons of revival in American history when God called a series of godly leaders in succession. For example, as Charles Finney was approaching the end of his career, God raised up Jeremiah Lanphier and then D. L. Moody. Yet there has been a long drought since the last great awakening occurred in America. While there are many wonderful ministries and churches today, America's previous great awakenings are a distant memory. God's people must ask what it will take for God to revive His people once more. What price must be paid for the Holy Spirit to turn the church back to Him? Who is willing to pay the price for revival?

What price do you think will need to be paid before revival comes to your church and spiritual awakening to your nation? Check all that apply.

[ ] Give up ineffective church programs.
[ ] Spend large amounts of time in corporate prayer.
[ ] Confront sinfulness in the church.
[ ] Honestly assess whether our hearts are faithful to God.
[ ] Personally repent of secret sin.
[ ] Other:

Why are there so few willing to pay the price required to be mightily used by God?

What price are you presently paying to serve God?

What price do you sense God wants you still to pay? Take a few moments to write down what you feel God is calling you to sacrifice so that He can use you to bring about revival and spiritual awakening.

7. People Filled with the Holy Spirit

A seventh characteristic of those God uses in revival is that they are filled with the Holy Spirit. From the moment of Pentecost, when the Holy Spirit descended in power, the church was never the same (see Acts 2). The preaching on that day was so compelling that three thousand people believed the gospel and were baptized. The city could not ignore the early Christians, because the power of the Holy Spirit was evident in all they did. Being filled with the Holy Spirit, ordinary Christians had great boldness and exerted enormous influence on the city (see Acts 4:31).

What does it mean to be filled with the Spirit? It is complete surrender to God's activity in your life and divine empowerment to follow His commands. Paul wrote in Ephesians 5:18, "Don't get drunk with wine, which leads to reckless actions, but be filled with the Spirit." The emphasis in the original language is for a continual filling of the Spirit. It is not a once-in-a-lifetime activity, and then we never need to seek the Spirit's presence again. Rather, we must be desperate for a daily filling by the Spirit in our lives.

When believers are filled with the Spirit, God's hand is on everything they do. Their preaching is done in power. Their testimonies bring deep conviction. Their service builds up the church body. Conversely, years of toil, without the Holy Spirit's filling, are futile.

"When they had prayed, the place where they were assembled was shaken, and they were all filled with the Holy Spirit and began to speak God's message with boldness."
Acts 4:31

Desperate for the Spirit's Filling

Duncan Campbell served as a respectable pastor in Scotland for 17 years but saw minimal spiritual fruit from his labor. Finally, he could stand it no longer. Duncan spent several hours crying out for God's presence until suddenly God answered his prayer at five o'clock in the morning. Campbell later recalled, "As I lay there, God the Holy Ghost came upon me. Wave after wave came rolling over me until the love of God swept through me like a mighty river."[22] From that point onward God used Campbell in revival wherever he went. Only after he grew desperate to be filled with the Spirit did his walk with God reach an entirely new level of intimacy and power.

When you read the sermon transcripts from many of the great revivals, you might be amazed by the lack of oratorical skill displayed by the preachers. Knowing that hundreds and even thousands of people were spiritually awakened when the sermon was originally preached, it can be disappointing to read a message that appears so ordinary. However, words on a page cannot convey the supercharged atmosphere that filled the room as the Holy Spirit brought conviction to the people in attendance. Even the most mundane words and actions become powerful, overwhelming divine instruments when the Holy Spirit chooses to use them.

Are You Filled with the Holy Spirit?

The filling of the Holy Spirit enables you to accomplish God's assignments. Never take the Spirit's filling for granted. Every Christian has the Holy Spirit residing within, but His filling is another matter (see Acts 4:31). Just because you walked closely with the Lord last week and were powerfully filled with His Spirit does not mean the same is true today. The Spirit's filling must be constantly renewed. Those who have been used mightily in revival are those who have been filled with the Spirit. Those who have maintained a state of renewal are those who have heeded Paul's injunction to be daily filled anew with the Spirit. Be advised: you cannot fill yourself! You can only submit yourself to the Lord so that He fills you with His Spirit.

Describe a time when you knew the Holy Spirit enabled you to do something you could not accomplish apart from His power.

The Spirit's filling must be constantly renewed.

List ways the Holy Spirit can work through faithful believers to revive the church.

Again, the key to being filled with the Holy Spirit's presence is to completely surrender your life to Him. Take time to yield every aspect of your life to Him so that the Spirit has access to all of your life today.

Encountering God in Prayer and Action

As the Lord of your life, God expects to exercise His rule over every part of your life. As you pray, wholly surrender yourself afresh to Christ: your thoughts, actions, attitudes, weaknesses, strengths, fears, desires, relationships, past, future, goals, and sins. Every area of your life that is cleansed and welcoming to the Holy Spirit is one more area where the Holy Spirit will now rule and use for His glory.

Day 5 # God Uses People Who Give Him the Glory

Stealing God's Glory

C. L. Culpepper was a missionary to China during the great Shantung Revival. The revival started when the Holy Spirit began convicting the missionaries of their sin. The missionaries had made great sacrifices to serve in China, and many of them had become frustrated because their work among the Chinese nationals had not delivered greater results. But as the Holy Spirit began to convict them, they came to see the reasons for the barrenness of many of their ministries. C. L. Culpepper confessed:

> "The Holy Spirit and God's Word continued to probe until I believed I would die under the searching, accusing finger of God. I still could not go to bed; so I went upstairs, called my wife, and asked her to come downstairs and pray with me. We prayed for a long time, then got up at 5:00 for the early morning prayer meeting.
>
> "Immediately upon my arrival at the meeting place, I asked the leader to let me make a statement. I don't remember all that I said, but I know the Lord enabled me to tell my inner feelings to the group of 40 gathered there. I told them how God had made me realize my spiritual impotence. I told my missionary colleagues that their praise of me as being a good missionary had made me proud. I told my Chinese coworkers ... I had stolen God's glory. My heart was so broken, I didn't believe I could live any longer."[23]

Culpepper realized that even as he attempted to serve the Lord, his pride had grown and robbed him of the Spirit's power. As soon as he renounced that sin and focused all the glory back on his Lord, God began using him powerfully as a divine instrument for revival.

8. People Who Give Glory to God

There are many reasons someone might desire revival. Perhaps it is to see church attendance increase, offerings grow, troublemakers repent, or the church and its minister gain a reputation in the Christian community. Human pride has a way of inserting itself into the most hallowed places. Even if the motivation is not bad, per se, there is really only one valid reason to desire revival—for God's glory. Revival is about the glory of God.

Brian Edwards said, "Those whom God uses in leadership in revival are always men who have met with God in a powerfully personal way and have a burning passion for the glory of God and a life of holiness."[24] Revival occurs when people see God as He is and recognize themselves for what they are. It is when God has the proper place in our lives, in the life of our church, and in our nation. Therefore, those God uses in revival must be men and women who readily give all the glory to God.

Why are some people tempted to steal glory from God?

What are some ways we can rob God of His glory?

"I had stolen God's glory."
—C. L. Culpepper

Revival is about the glory of God.

What are some lessons you have learned in this study that you can use to guard your heart from intruding on God's glory?

Wanting God to Be Glorified

The Korean Revival of 1907 began in large part with missionaries who had heard of the recent outpouring of God's Spirit in India.[25] The church leaders in Korea saw what God was capable of doing among people in another region in the world and then wept that He had not done the same in their land. They longed for God to be honored in their country in the same way He was being magnified in India. Those who want God to be exalted in their lives and in their church can be certain of God's active support of their efforts. However, when people begin to covet what belongs to God alone, we place ourselves in opposition to the Holy Spirit.

During the First Great Awakening James Davenport cherished the limelight that great men such as George Whitefield and Jonathan Edwards were experiencing. As a result, the Spirit withdrew His blessing and Davenport experienced humiliation. David Matthews suggested that Evan Roberts became such a celebrity during the Welsh Revival that when people began to honor him in too great a measure, it was time for him to step aside.[26] Though it was never Roberts's desire to rob God of His honor, times of revival bring temptations to leaders as well as to congregations. A priority for anyone involved in revival is to diligently and fervently keep their efforts God-focused and God-honoring. Effective catalysts for revival are people who bring glory solely to God in all they do.

However, when people begin to covet what belongs to God alone, we place ourselves in opposition to the Holy Spirit.

Catalysts for Revival
1. **People who are ordinary**
2. **People with a passion for God**
3. **People committed to God's Word.**
4. **People committed to prayer**
5. **People committed to working with others**
6. **People willing to pay the price**
7. **People who are filled with the Holy Spirit**
8. **People who give God the glory**

Review the eight characteristics in the box. Which of them do you sense God wants to develop in your life so that He can use you to bring revival to people around you?

Influencing Your Church for Revival

God is looking for those who will stand in the gap on behalf of others. It is a high calling. Such an assignment requires divinely mandated qualifications. We pray that a growing number of people would be willing to pay any price to be used in whatever ways God chooses so that revival would come. God's people cannot continue doing business as usual and expect something extraordinary to occur. For an extraordinary work to happen, our commitment and the caliber of our walk with God must also be extraordinary. We hope you have taken a major step in that direction as you have completed this study.

Over the past six weeks you have been exposed to extensive teaching on revival. You have heard the stories of those God powerfully used to draw the church back to God. You have read about how God worked to transform sinners into saints, to awaken lethargic churches, and to powerfully impact entire nations. But all of this information will be useless to you unless your life is changed as a result of this study.

You can do some simple things to make a profound impact on your church.

1. Review what God said to you during this study.
List every promise you encountered in His Word. Keep that list in your Bible and regularly review it. Pray over it until every one of those promises becomes a reality in your life and church.

> **Write down the lesson you've learned that is taking top priority in your life right now.**

2. List every commitment and action you sense God wants you to take.
Keep that list before you also. Allow no excuses or delays. Take immediate action until you are doing everything you told God you would do. Never take a commitment to God lightly (see Ecclesiastes 5:4-5).

> **Write down the commitments God has called you to make through this study.**

3. Find another believer or a small group who will hold you accountable to follow through with what God told you during this course.

You are not serious about revival if you are not willing to make yourself accountable to others. Regularly meet with these people to pray and share updates on what God is doing.

> **Who are the people you trust to hold you accountable for fulfilling a commitment to seek revival in your own life and in your church?**

We pray that a growing number of people would be willing to pay any price to be used in whatever ways God chooses so that revival would come.

4. Continue to study God's Word, especially passages that speak about revival.

Let Scripture become more to you than merely words on a page. Let the truths you find in the Bible's pages become realities in your life.

> **What Scripture passages from this study has God used to teach you new lessons or to lead you to obey old ones?**

5. Prepare yourself for opposition.

The only thing on earth Satan despises more than God's people is God's people when they are revived and on fire for God. Expect opposition and criticism. Cling to the Holy Spirit and allow Him to be your strength and guide during the difficult times that will inevitably come.

> **How will you prepare for the spiritual battles that lie ahead?**
>
> [ ] **Read the Bible regularly.**
> [ ] **Pray more passionately.**
> [ ] **Become watchful regarding temptation.**
> [ ] **Ask another believer to hold me accountable to my commitments.**
> [ ] **Other:**

6. Stay spiritually alert.

Now that you have studied how revival works, watch for it in your life and church. It may be much closer than you imagined!

> **As you have become more alert during the course of this study, what signs of spiritual decay have you noticed in our churches or country?**

> **What are the signs of God's movement to bring revival to the church?**

> **How do you perceive that God wants to use you as a catalyst for revival and spiritual awakening?**

Thank you for taking time to study this material on the crucial subject of revival. We hope that God will use it to turn His people back to Himself and that revival will burst forth wherever it is studied. This is a day that desperately cries out for revival.

Will you be someone God will use to bring a spirit of refreshing to His people and a powerful, nationwide awakening across the land?

Encountering God in Prayer and Action

Conclude this study with a sincere prayer of surrender and commitment to God. Release any pride that may have hindered you from fully serving God or from giving Him all the glory. Ask God to take all you have learned and move it from your head to your heart. Pray that God uses your life to be a catalyst for revival. Pray that God's work of revival will begin in you so that it can spread to others.

This is a day that desperately cries out for revival.

1. Jessie Penn-Lewis, *The Awakening in Wales (And Some of the Hidden Springs)* (England: Overcomer Publications, n.d.), 39.
2. Richard Owen Roberts, ed., *Scotland Saw His Glory* (Wheaton, IL: International Awakening Press, 1995), 115.
3. Ibid., 116-117.
4. Brian Edwards, *Revival! A People Saturated with God* (Durham, England: Evangelical Press, 1995), 50.
5. Thomas Phillips, *The Welsh Revival: Its Origin and Development* (Pennsylvania: The Banner of Truth Trust, 1989), 132.
6. Brian Edwards, *Revival!,* 48.
7. James Alexander Stewart, *William Chambers Burns, Robert Murray McCheyne* (Alexandria, LA: Lamplighter Publications, n.d.), 19.
8. Ibid.
9. Arthur Wallis, *In the Day of Your Power: A Picture of Revival from Scripture and History* (Columbia, MO: City Hill Publishing, 1990), xi.
10. James Alexander Stewart, *William Chambers Burns, Robert Murray McCheyne*, 12.
11. Malcom McDow and Alvin Reid, *Firefall: How God Has Shaped History Through Revivals* (Nashville: B&H Publishing Group, 1997), 278.
12. Wallis, *In the Day of Your Power*, 118.
13. D. Macfarlan, *The Revivals of the Eighteenth Century, Particularly at Cambuslang* (Wheaton, IL: Richard Owen Roberts Publishers, 1980), 11.
14. McDow and Reid, *Firefall*, 213.
15. J. C. Pollock, *Moody: A Biographical Portrait of the Pacesetter in Modern Mass Evangelism* (New York: The Macmillan Company, 1963), 99.
16. Duncan Campbell, *The Price and Power of Revival* (Fort Washington, PA: Christian Literature Crusade, n.d.), 43–45.
17. Brian Edwards, *Revival!,* 50.
18. Jonathan Goforth, *By My Spirit* (Grand Rapids: Zondervan Publishing House, 1942), 19.
19. J. Oswald Sanders, *Spiritual Leadership: Principles of Excellence for Every Believer* (Chicago: Moody Press, 1994), 119.
20. David Matthews, *I Saw the Welsh Revival*, (Chicago: Moody Press, 1951), 19.
21. Andrew Bonar, *Robert Murray M'Cheyne: Memoirs and Remains* (Carlisle, PA: Banner of Truth, 1960), 143.
22. Duncan Campbell, *The Nature of a God-Sent Revival* (Christ Life Publications, n.d.), 25.
23. C. L. Culpepper, *The Shantung Revival* (n.p., n.d.), 29.
24. Brian Edwards, *Revival!,* 48.
25. Jonathan Goforth, *When the Spirit's Fire Swept Korea* (Grand Rapids: Zondervan Publishing House, 1958), 16.
26. Matthews, *I Saw the Welsh Revival*, 74.

Session 6
Small-Group Discussion Guide

Open in prayer.

Ahead of time, ask someone to be prepared to pray. Invite prayer requests and ask the group for prayer requests that pertain to personal and corporate revival. Listen for how God is presently working in their lives through the study so that the group will know how to pray for them. Once people have had an opportunity to share, call on the person appointed to pray.

View Session 6 of the Teaching DVD

Truths to Remember

Scriptures to Read

Quotes to Remember

Actions to Take

If you missed this session, go to *www.lifeway.com/freshencounter* to download this and any other session of *Fresh Encounter.*

Discussion Guide

Ask group members what the most challenging truth was that they encountered this past week.

Which of the eight characteristics of a catalyst for revival most challenged you?

Have you ever seen yourself as a potential catalyst for revival? Why or why not?

Ask group members to respond to what they heard on the DVD.

Why does God seem to most often use "ordinary people" to serve as the catalysts for revival?

Reflect on the encounter Jesus had with the Samaritan woman at the well in John 4:1-42.

What did the woman do once she understood Jesus' true identity?

Describe the effect her transformed life had on her hometown (v. 39-42).

In the video, Richard said, "One changed life is all it takes for a movement to begin."

Having come face-to-face with God and His truth during this study, what changes are necessary for you to have a closer walk with God?

What needs to be developed in your life for God to use you in a greater way as a catalyst for revival?

When confronted with the apathy of members in his congregation, Evan Roberts prayer was not for them. Ultimately, he prayed, "O Lord, bend me." Describe the results if an entire congregation began to express this attitude in prayer.

In the video, Henry taught that believers must stop asking what we need to do in order to bring revival. Instead, Christians should seek to understand what God is doing.

What is God doing in these arenas that indicate His desire to bring about revival?

Your life

The life of your church

The life of your community

Ask members to share a single prayer request each member can pray for the others in the coming days. Ask them to finish the statement:

"In light of what God has taught me about revival, please pray that in the coming days I ..."

Close in prayer.

Fresh Encounter
Leader Helps

༺ † ༻

Thank you for serving as a leader and facilitator in the *Fresh Encounter* study! We hope that you will move through the next seven weeks with a great expectancy for what God will do in your group, church, and community.

Please take a few minutes to review the following encouragements and instructions to make *Fresh Encounter* as effective as possible for your group.

1. Getting Started with the Introductory Session

For this study, we have given you an introductory session to get the group started. For your first gathering, the goals are simple:

→ **Pass out the workbooks**
→ **Watch the Introductory Session DVD segment**
→ **Get acquainted with one another**
→ **Instill expectancy in the group**

As the group leader, this session gives you an opportunity to set the pace for the next six weeks. During the first gathering, take time to listen closely to members' backgrounds and views about revivals. By understanding the perspective of the group members, you will better know how to lead the group and pray for each of them. Also, make sure to share your own excitement about what the Lord can do in the group and through the church over the next six weeks.

2. Prayer is Essential.

We believe prayer is so vital for the church to be revived that we have included an entire session on it. In order for you to properly lead the *Fresh Encounter* study, your prayer life is critical. Your first order of business should be to pray for your own walk with Christ to reflect a revived relationship. Each week, test your understanding and actions to see if they reflect the truths of this study.

Another activity you should engage with is to pray daily for the members of your group.

In the space below, list the members of your group:

_____	_____
_____	_____
_____	_____
_____	_____

In order to best lead your group, commit to pray for them daily as a part of your own homework and preparation to lead this study.

3. Build Community

God's intention is to revive believers and build His church. *Fresh Encounter* is designed so that a person could learn the material on an individual basis but it is most effective when done with a group. As your group moves through the material, please emphasize two principles with them: accountability and confidentiality.

The very nature of the subject matter for *Fresh Encounter* calls for accountability among believers. As you prepare each week to lead the group discussion, think through how you can ask insightful questions and elicit honest responses. Encourage the group members to recite the memory verse when appropriate in the discussions. Ask pointed questions regarding the homework from the book.

Also necessary for this study is confidentiality. Hopefully, members of your group will share about how God is personally challenging and changing their lives. It is possible that a time of mutual confession of sin may occur in your group. Show sensitivity to your group members by encouraging and modeling confidentiality about what is shared during the group discussions.

4. Prepare

To be an effective leader, you must be prepared for the group sessions. It is easy to be prepared if you will do three simple things. First, complete all of the homework for each session. Make sure you have thoroughly thought through all of the truths presented in the daily work. Second, watch the DVD segment prior to gathering. By becoming familiar with the video teaching, you will be better prepared to discuss both the truths as they stand and how God is shaping your own life with these truths.

Finally, read all the group session material ahead of time. Because of your personal knowledge of your group, there may be certain questions you wish to adjust, replace, or highlight. By studying the group session guide before the meeting, you can pray for God's guidance in how to lead the discussion.

5. Leading the Session

At the end of the homework for each session is the Small-Group Discussion Guide. Included on the first page is a suggestion for how to open the gathering time with a time of prayer. Please do not feel the need to rush through the opening prayer time. Instead, as the leader, listen closely for the ways God is working in the lives of your friends. As they talk about the needs in their lives, you will the have the opportunity to help them see how God might be calling them to a fresh encounter with Him.

Next is a Listening Guide while your group views the DVD. It includes headings where notes can be made from the teaching on the DVD. As you watch the DVD beforehand and during the session, make note of truths, Scriptures, quotes, and actions that can be discussed after viewing the DVD. Each week, remind your participants that they can go to *www.lifeway.com* to view any of the *Fresh Encounter* videos online.

Once you have finished viewing the DVD teaching session, move into your group discussion using the second page of the Small-Group Discussion Guide. The questions are here to aid your group in understanding the biblical truths about revival and spiritual awakening. However, there may be other issues that are important for your group to discuss which are not included in the questions provided. We would prefer that you be sensitive to the Holy Spirit's leading rather than feel constrained by the questions provided. Please use the questions as a guide to help move your group toward a fresh encounter with God.

Once again, we want to thank you for making the commitment to lead a group through *Fresh Encounter*. Our prayer is that God will use this study to bring revival to your church and a spiritual awakening to your community.

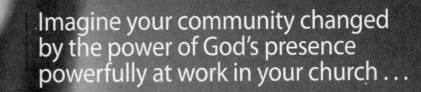

Imagine your community changed by the power of God's presence powerfully at work in your church . . .

Revival is undoubtedly needed in the church today. Our culture desperately needs a spiritual awakening. And God is waiting for His people to cry to Him for it. Because when they do, the joy of revival will come and life will be refreshed. *Fresh Encounter* is a seven-session study that will challenge believers to examine their lives and return to their first love—Christ. Join Henry and Richard Blackaby as they lead this small-group study to examine the Scriptures about His intention to revive the church and see it become a catalyst for spiritual awakening. Order the study online, call 800.458.2772, or visit the LifeWay Christian Store serving you.

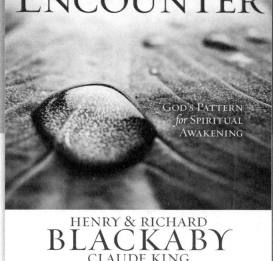

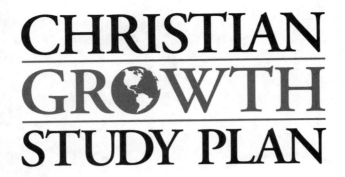

CHRISTIAN GROWTH STUDY PLAN

In the Christian Growth Study Plan, *Fresh Encounter* is a resource for course credit in the subject area Personal Life in the Christian Growth category of plans. To receive credit, read the book; complete the learning activities; attend group sessions; show your work to your pastor, a staff member, or a church leader; then complete this form. This page may be duplicated. Send the completed page to:

Christian Growth Study Plan; One LifeWay Plaza; Nashville, TN 37234-0117; Fax (615) 251-5067; e-mail *cgspnet@lifeway.com.* For more about the plan, refer to the current *Christian Growth Study Plan Catalog,* located online at *www.lifeway.com/cgsp.* If you do not have access to the Internet, contact the Christian Growth Study Plan office, (800) 968-5519, for the specific plan you need for your ministry.

Fresh Encounter • Course Number: CG-0117

PARTICIPANT INFORMATION

Social Security Number (USA ONLY-optional) _ _ _

Personal CGSP Number* _ _

Date of Birth (MONTH, DAY, YEAR) _ _

Name (First, Middle, Last)

Home Phone _ _

Address (Street, Route, or P.O. Box)

City, State, or Province

Zip/Postal Code

Email Address for CGSP use

Please check appropriate box: ☐ Resource purchased by church ☐ Resource purchased by self ☐ Other

CHURCH INFORMATION

Church Name

Address (Street, Route, or P.O. Box)

City, State, or Province

Zip/Postal Code

CHANGE REQUEST ONLY

☐ Former Name

☐ Former Address

City, State, or Province

Zip/Postal Code

☐ Former Church

City, State, or Province

Zip/Postal Code

Signature of Pastor, Conference Leader, or Other Church Leader

Date

*New participants are requested but not required to give SS# and date of birth. Existing participants, please give CGSP# when using SS# for the first time. Thereafter, only one ID# is required. **Mail to:** Christian Growth Study Plan, One LifeWay Plaza, Nashville, TN 37234-0117. Fax: (615)251-5067.

Revised 4-05